MINI MAKERS

MINI MAKERS

Crafty makes to create with your kids

Laura Minter & Tia Williams

First published 2016 by Guild of Master Craftsman
Publications Ltd, Castle Place, 166 High Street, Lewes,
East Sussex, BN7 1XU

ISBN 978 1 78494 101 7

A catalogue record for this book is available from
the British Library.

Publisher Jonathan Bailey
Production Manager Jim Bulley
Senior Project Editor Virginia Brehaut
Managing Art Editor Gilda Pacitti
Art Editor Rebecca Mothersole
Photographers Emma Sekhon, Rebecca Mothersole
Step-by-step photographs by Laura Minter
and Tia Williams

Colour origination by GMC Reprographics
Printed and bound in China

For our Little Buttons, Harper and Amelie

Contents

Introduction

Putting your aprons on, rolling up your sleeves and getting crafty with kids is so important. Even from a young age, art can help children express themselves, to show their emotions and thoughts and to explore their favourite things before they are able to fully communicate through language. Art develops a whole range of motor skills, from holding paintbrushes and using scissors to mastering a needle and thread. It's also a brilliant way to fill up rainy days and bust boredom. We know (*we know!*) it can be really hard to think of ways to occupy children – they get bored easily, their tastes change quickly and they are hard to entertain. But there are so many crafting activities to try that it soon becomes easy to keep their attention. Plus, crafting with kids doesn't require elaborate materials or cost much money, is a great way to recycle and doesn't need much skill to get started. Win!

Designed with crafting and play both firmly in mind, most of the makes in this book are structured to allow adults to create the foundation, with the child embellishing and personalizing the end product. This means that the crafts are sturdy and should stand the test of time, while giving the children something they can feel proud of. Learning through play is a theme throughout. Each project describes a range of ideas for how to develop the activities further, with suggestions for how to play with and adapt the makes.

These projects are suitable for girls and boys aged three and upwards, but wherever possible we suggest ways in which they can be altered or extended to suit younger children. They are aimed at beginner crafters and all of them should be easy, even if you've never picked up a paintbrush before. Also included are five sections to give you extra information, advice and ideas on different craft techniques.

You really don't need any super skills to enjoy crafting together. Kids will love the things you make with them *because* you made them with them. They will be unique, personal and the fun you had creating them will be remembered. It doesn't matter if the end result looks different to the photographs in this book. Let your kids be as creative as they like and bear in mind that the process is just as important as the product.

Kids' Craft Kit

This section provides an overview of the basic supplies recommended for the projects in this book. Most of the materials can be purchased easily in craft shops or online. For more details, see the list of suppliers on page 157.

Keep a craft stash

It's a really good idea to build up a stock of the things you may need. Find a corner in your kitchen or garage and fill a big box with containers, card, fabric scraps and anything else you come across that could be turned into something great. Using up things that would otherwise end up in a rubbish bin helps to reduce waste, saves money and gives children a valuable lesson in recycling.

Here are some ideas of things to keep hold of: Old items of clothing, sheets and other fabrics can be chopped up and turned into something. Even tiny scraps are great for making collages. Cardboard tubes and plastic pots can be turned into telescopes, toy cars, robots or anything your imagination can conjure up. Keep large boxes for turning into houses, boats and life-sized cut-outs of your kids! Bottle tops, beads and buttons make perfect switches, decorations and facial features.

Art and craft supplies

With a good array of stuff saved from the bin, you will also need to arm yourself with a few key supplies. These don't cost a lot and your stocks can evolve gradually as you need them. Make sure you have basic items such as a ruler, scissors, hole punch, craft knife, pencils (graphite and colouring) and felt-tip pens. These items are essential for loads of craft projects so if you don't have them it would be a good idea to stock up.

Adhesives

Glue (PVA, glue sticks and strong glue), duct tape (which is super strong), masking tape and decorative tape are all great for crafting. We've also used mini duct tape to embellish projects but this could be substituted with washi tape, both of which are readily available online or in craft stores.

Card, paper and foam

Having a good variety of coloured card, paper and craft foam is very handy and most craft stores stock mixed packs.

Paint and brushes

A range of paint colours is a must for any craft kit. Child-friendly paints tend to be runnier, so will need several coats to get a vivid, even coverage. When we're not painting with children we use acrylic paint because it has a more hard-wearing coverage. You can also buy acrylic spray paint, which is fantastic for covering most surfaces. A range of different-sized brushes is useful. Give a selection to kids when they are painting too as they love the variation.

Paper plates

These can be purchased in large packs really cheaply. There are so many things you can make from them. We use them for the Stitched Sun and Moon (page 122), the Paper-plate Tambourine (page 72 and to add portholes to the Foldaway Cardboard Boat (page 36).

Air-dry clay and polymer clay

These are fantastic additions to a craft kit. They are fun and easy to work with, even for little hands. Polymer clay comes in a large variety of colours and air-dry clay can be painted. For a cheaper alternative to these, salt dough is also great (see the recipe on page 146) but bear in mind that it isn't as easy to mould, so keep your shapes and structures basic.

Sewing equipment

We use a sewing machine for speed and accuracy, but the sewing projects in this book don't rely on the use of a machine. Pins, needles, a variety of threads, fabric scissors and tailor's chalk are all essential sewing items.

Plastic needle and threads

Yarn, ribbon or embroidery thread are all great for introducing kids to sewing and improving hand-eye coordination. Children's plastic sewing needles can be bought as a safer alternative to metal ones.

Fabrics

Felt and fleece are wonderful beginner fabrics as they come in a variety of colours and do not fray, meaning you can leave the edges unsewn. Felt is great for children because it's cheap and easy for little hands to work with.

Trims and accessories

Having a well-stocked box of buttons, beads, ribbons, rickrack, pompoms, sequins and gems will come in handy for adding finishing touches to a project. Pipe cleaners are wonderful for creating shape and dimension and can be used to make anything from crowns and butterflies to Christmas decorations.

Crafting Safely with Children

Crafting with children is incredibly fun, messy and inventive. But please remember that supervision from an adult is needed all the way through to help mini makers create their masterpieces and keep them safe. The projects in this book have elements that are designed to be done by your children, but there are also parts that should only be undertaken by an adult, for safety reasons.

Where possible, we have opted for the most child-friendly craft supplies and practices, but sometimes using more grown-up materials is needed, to be able to create an end product that will stand the test of time and children. Below are a few guidelines for safety when working on the projects within this book. Some of them may seem obvious, but it's easy to get distracted with kids, to let your guard down, or to leave the room without certain considerations. So safety is always worth a second thought!

Paints

Most of the projects use poster or acrylic paint, which is fine for a child to use with supervision. A few projects, including the Foldaway Cardboard Boat on page 36 and the Recycled Drum Kit on page 76 call for painting metals and plastic surfaces. Acrylic spray paint is really the best option here to adhere to the surfaces well with an even coverage. Spray painting creates fumes and should only be done by an adult in a very well ventilated area and away from any fire. Always check the guidelines on the aerosol can before using.

Dangerous objects

Plastic, child-friendly scissors can be used to cut paper and card, but sharper scissors or a craft knife will be needed to cut cardboard for the Foldaway Cardboard Boat on page 36, the Cardboard Anchor on page 42 and the magnetic sheets for the Magnetic Family Faces on page 16. This must be done by an adult.

A hot iron is required for the Easy Royal Robe project on page 143. Make sure children are kept away from it and do not leave it unattended on the ironing board to avoid the risk of the cable being pulled.

Keep craft tools on a high shelf, out of reach. Hammers and nails (for the Dancing Family Puppets on page 108) should also be used carefully, away from little fingers.

Glue

For durability and a quicker drying time, we use strong, non-toxic glue. Using a glue stick or PVA glue is great for kids to stick card and paper but something stronger is needed for many of the projects, and these parts must be done by an adult.

Choking hazards

When crafting with younger children, be aware of the smaller craft materials and the risk of them being put into mouths.

Baking

We have selected baking projects that are suitable for children to do with adults and neither recipe calls for the use of a sharp knife. Use plastic bowls and keep children well away from sharp knives and any source of heat.

Rainy-day Games

When the rain is drizzling and the kids are bored, these makes are the perfect antidote. The Family Fishing Game, Pebble Dominoes and Magnetic Family Faces are all fun games designed to teach basic numeracy skills through scoring and number recognition.

SKILLS LEARNED:
SHARING, FOLLOWING INSTRUCTIONS,
GAME PLAYING, NUMERACY, PAINTING,
CUTTING AND STICKING

Magnetic Family Faces

These magnetic family faces are a great way to make your family look wonderfully silly. Made from photographs glued onto magnetic sheets and adorned with accessories, this game will keep kids entertained and amused for ages. They will love designing and colouring in crazy accessories to dress up the faces – and when they get bored of the current faces they can create more to keep the activity fresh.

You will need

- Digital camera

- Access to a computer and colour printer

- 4 x sheets of photographic paper

- 7 x magnetic sheets, measuring 8 x 12in (20 x 30cm)

- 4 x sheets of paper in pastel colours, 8 x 12in (20 x 30cm)

- 4 x sheets of white card, 8 x 12in (20 x 30cm)

- Number stickers

- Gold acrylic paint and paintbrush

- Strong glue

- Felt-tip pens in a variety of colours

- Ruler

- Pencil

- Scissors

- Dice

- Templates for the accessories, found on page 154

1 Begin by taking a headshot of each family member with a digital camera. Upload to a computer and print them out onto photographic paper so that each face measures approximately 5in (12.5cm) high by 4in (10cm) wide. To get the right size, resize your photos and print out testers on normal paper.

2 Roughly cut out each face and then glue it onto the unmagnetized side of a magnetic sheet. Gently smooth out any air bubbles with your fingers. Before gluing, test which is the magnetic side by placing it against a radiator or fridge.

3 When the glue has dried, cut neatly around the outline of the face, ears and hair.

4 Place the ruler onto each face and use a pencil to draw faint lines dividing the forehead, eyes, nose and mouth into four sections. Cut these out.

5 Photocopy and cut out the features and accessories from page 154, or draw your own. Colour them in with felt-tip pens and then follow Steps 2 and 3 to add the magnetic backing.

6 Turn all the pieces over so that they are face down, with the magnetic side up. Stick the number stickers (only numbers between 1 and 6) on the back of each.

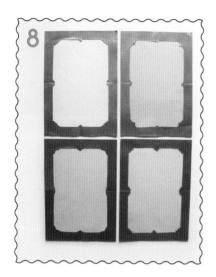

Let's play!

How to play magnetic family faces

This game is for two or more players. Turn all the pieces number side up and give each player a magnetic board. Take it in turns to roll the dice, select a piece (with corresponding number to that rolled on the dice) and add it to your board. Build up the face first, if you can, then add the features. If you roll the dice and there are no pieces available, you can either swap an existing piece or skip a turn. The winner is the player who first completes a full face with four accessories added to it.

You can also enjoy playing with the pieces to create silly portraits of your family. With another player, see who can make each family member look the silliest with accessories in the shortest time. Young children can piece the faces together like a jigsaw puzzle and enjoy naming their family members.

7 To make the framed boards, take a piece of white card and fold it in quarters. Draw a border around the two unfolded edges, about 1in (2.5cm) from the edge. Then add some details to the corner. Repeat three more times on the other pieces of card. Use scissors to cut along the lines on each piece of folded card, then open them up to reveal a frame shape.

Let's make!

You can add more and more faces, features and accessories to this game. Why not include grandparents, cousins or even pets? You don't even need to stop at faces! For an alternative game, use photos of the whole body and draw different outfits to dress them up in.

8 Paint each frame piece with gold paint. Glue the four pastel sheets of paper onto the magnetic side of the four remaining magnetic sheets. Then glue the gold frames on top.

Children love to play about with pictures of themselves and their family, which is why projects like this (and the puppets on page 108) are always popular. For tiny tots, you could glue family photos onto wooden blocks to be stacked into a tower and then knocked down again. Mix up the photos with letters, numbers or patterns on each side of the blocks for a variety of things to stack.

Pebble Dominoes

Dominoes is an easy game to play and perfect for practicing counting and learning about patterns. These colourful pebbles are a modern twist on the classic game. Each pebble is painted with two different colours, with dot numbers painted on one side. Younger children can use the sides with no numbers and match up just the colours. Older children can play the more advanced number-matching version (see page 25 for full instructions).

You will need

For the dominoes

- 21 pebbles, roughly 2in (5cm) in length
- White, green, yellow, blue and black acrylic paint
- Paintbrush
- Masking tape
- Pencil with a rubber on the end
- An old plate

For the bag

- Small canvas drawstring bag, 6 x 8in (15 x 20cm)
- Fabric paints in four contrasting colours
- Black marker pen
- 2 x paintbrushes
- An old plate
- Medium-sized potato
- Craft knife
- A few sheets of kitchen towel
- Domino templates, found on page 156
- Piece of paper

1 Begin by washing the pebbles and drying them thoroughly. Wrap a strip of masking tape neatly halfway around a pebble and completely cover one half of it with tape. Repeat for all the pebbles, making sure the tape is properly stuck down.

2 Paint the sides of the pebbles that aren't taped with white, green, yellow and blue acrylic paint, ensuring a roughly even mix of colours. You may need several coats of paint for an even coverage. Once the pebbles are completely dry, remove the masking tape.

3 Place another strip of masking tape over the painted side, aligning it closely to the edge of the paint.

4 Then paint the other side of each pebble with all the colours, ensuring a roughly even mix of colours. Do not paint any dominoes the same colour as the existing half. When completely dry, remove the masking tape.

5 Load a little black paint onto a plate. Using a pencil with a rubber on the end, dip the rubber into the paint. On a piece of scrap paper, test out making black dots. When you are happy with the technique, stamp dots carefully onto the pebbles. You can also copy the pattern of dots on a dice. Range the dots from 1 to 6, ensuring there is an even mix of numbers across the pebbles. There should be seven of each number in total.

6 To make the potato-print bag, photocopy and cut out the domino templates from page 156. Cut the potato in half across the width and place the templates on each cut side of the potato. Use a sharp pencil to draw around them onto the potato, making a groove all the way around.

7 Remove the template and use a craft knife to cut around the pencil groove so that the stamp outline is about ¼in (6mm) deep.

8 Lay the potato on its side and slice into it, ¼in (6mm) deeper than the cut edge. Carefully slice away the potato surrounding the image.

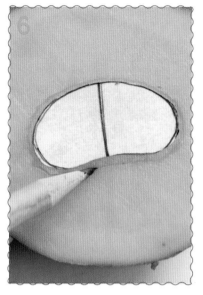

9 Lay the template back onto the potato and use the craft knife to cut across the indicated lines. Remove the potato from between the lines. Repeat with the second template on the other half of the potato.

10 Place a piece of paper inside the canvas bag (to prevent the paint from seeping through to the other side). Squeeze the four colours of fabric paint onto the plate. Dab the potato with kitchen towel to remove any moisture then paint the two sides of one of the stamps with different colours, using a separate brush for each.

11 Stamp the potato onto the bag, carefully pressing down and giving it a little wiggle to make sure there are no gaps in the print. Repaint the potato stamp and then repeat, to make four prints on the bag.

12 Wash the brushes and paint the other half of the potato with the remaining two colours. Then stamp another four dominos onto your bag. Leave the paint to dry. Repeat steps 11 and 12 on the other side of the bag. Add dotted numbers to the dominoes using a black marker pen, with the paper in the middle to stop the pen going through.

Let's play!

How to play dominoes

This game is for two to four players. Each player is given four dominoes at random, leaving any remaining pebbles in the middle to draw from. The youngest player starts by putting one of their dominoes onto the table. Then, the next player must select one of their dominoes that has at least one side matching the one on the table (in colour or number, depending on which version you play). Each time you put a domino down, you can pick up another from the draw pile. Keep going, forming a line with the dominoes. If you can't match any, skip a turn. The first player to play all their dominoes (or have the fewest remaining if no one can play) is the winner.

Let's make!

Pebbles are a great resource to use for games and learning. They're tactile and can be painted easily to create games. You could paint noughts and crosses on them to play tic-tac-toe. Use four crossed twigs to create the grid, then take turns to place the noughts or crosses in the grid to get three in a row. Painted pebbles are also great for storytelling. Create your own story stones by painting pebbles with pictures of people, places and objects for children to create fantastical stories. If you want to go beyond pebbles, why not make giant garden dominoes or tic-tac-toe by using cork placemats or coasters, which are really easy to paint.

Family Fishing Game

This multi-player fishing game is a perfect wet-weather activity. Cast your aquatic shapes over the edge of the sofa and get fishing. Each object has a different score, depending on how hard it is to pick up (the easier objects have more magnets embedded in them), and the game promotes maths skills because the children help to keep score as they play.

You will need

- 1 sheet each of 8 x 12in (20 x 30cm) felt in blue, yellow, pink, black, brown, orange and grey

- Scissors

- 15in (38cm) length of yellow ribbon, ¼in (6mm) wide

- 15in (38cm) length of green ribbon, ¼in (6mm) wide

- Black felt-tip pen

- 17 x magnets, ¼in (6mm) wide

- 22in (56cm) length of ½in (1cm) dowelling

- Bright pink and yellow acrylic paint

- Paintbrush

- 60in (150cm) yellow yarn

- 2½in (4cm) cardboard ribbon reel

- Strong glue

- 5 x sequins, ⅛in (3mm) in diameter

- Lollipop stick

- Small bead, ¼in (6mm) in diameter

- Templates for the fish, boot, treasure chest, treasure, jellyfish, shark, starfish and numbers found on page 155

1

2

3

4

Cutting-out tip

You can save time by roughly cutting out the fishing templates, then pinning them onto the felt, before cutting it all out more precisely with scissors. You could also layer up pieces of felt to cut out several of the same creatures in one go.

5

6

5 Glue the numbers onto one half of each of the felt pieces. The point system is as follows:

Boot = 1 point
Fish = 2 points
Jellyfish = 4 points
Starfish = 6 points
Shark = 8 points
Treasure chest = 10 points

6 Glue the magnets down on the centre of the back of the numbered pieces. Where applicable, spread them out so they are not all in one place and not too close to the edge. Glue three magnets onto the boot, two magnets onto the fish and jellyfish and one magnet onto each of the remaining pieces.

7 Attach the felt pairs to each other by adding a line of glue around the edges and carefully gluing them together. Leave to dry.

1 Photocopy and cut out the fishing templates found on page 155. You can also draw your own: make the shapes simple and around 4–5in (10–12cm) in size. For each object you will need to cut two pieces (one for the front and one for the back). Pin to the felt and cut out the following from each template:
4 x fish from blue felt
2 x boots from black felt
2 x treasure chest pieces from brown felt
1 x treasure piece from yellow felt
4 x jellyfish from pink felt
2 x sharks from grey felt
4 x starfish from yellow felt

2 For the jellyfish, cut 2½in (6cm) strips of ribbon in green and yellow. Cut six strips in green and six in yellow. Glue the ribbons, alternating in colour, onto the bottom of two of the jellyfish pieces, so that each one has three yellow and three green ribbons.

3 For the treasure chest, use a black pen to draw lines onto one of the pieces to create a chest shape, as shown on the template. Glue the yellow treasure on so that it looks like it is inside the chest. Once dry, glue a few sequins onto the yellow, so the treasure glistens.

4 Photocopy and cut out the number templates found on page 155. Cut out two each of the following numbers from felt: 1, 2, 4, and 6. Cut out one 0 and one 8 from felt. Pin the numbers to the orange felt and cut them out.

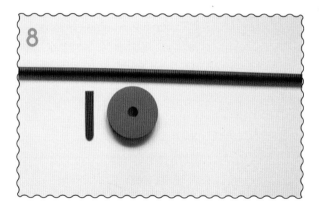

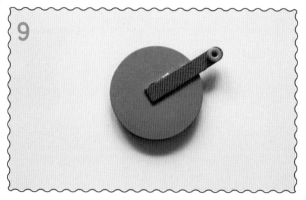

8 To make the rod, cut a lollipop stick in half with scissors so that it is about 2½in (6cm) long. Discard one of the halves and paint the other with bright pink paint. Paint the length of dowelling bright pink too and the cardboard ribbon reel yellow.

9 Glue the lollipop stick onto the reel, with the cut end of the stick covering the hole in the centre. Glue the bead onto the rounded end of the lollipop stick.

10 Cut a 2in (5cm) circle of yellow felt and place two magnets in the centre. Bundle the felt around the magnet then wrap the end of the yellow yarn around it a few times. Secure with a double knot and cut away the excess yarn.

11 Glue the reel to the rod 6in (15cm) from one end, using strong glue applied liberally. Leave to set completely. You may find it helps to secure a piece of tape over the reel to hold it in place while it sets.

12 Take the piece of yarn with the magnet at the bottom and tie it onto the end of the rod so that the magnet hangs about 20in (50cm) from the rod. Add a little glue to the knot to hold it in place. Now add glue all the way around the reel and, without pulling the yarn too tight, wrap the remaining yarn around the reel several times.

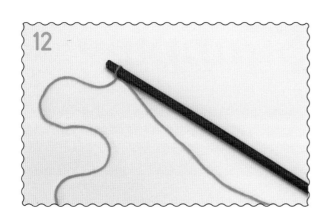

Let's play!

How to play family fishing

This game is for 2-4 players. Cast the objects onto the floor with the numbers facing down. Take it in turns to try and pick them up with the fishing rod. Whoever hooks the objects with the most points is the winner. This is great for developing balance, developing a steady hand and improving hand-eye coordination. Alternatively, you could see which player can pick up all the pieces in the quickest time. Encourage younger children to pick out selected colours and shapes rather than going for those with the highest score.

For more of a challenge, why not try hooking the shapes blindfolded? This is a great party game and you could even hide small chocolate coins or sweets under the fish for extra motivation.

Let's make!

You don't have to use felt for this project. If you prefer, you could cut the sea creatures from coloured scraps of card. Card won't be as resilient as felt, but kids will really enjoy drawing and colouring in the shapes. With card, you can make the shapes a little more elaborate too, so you could add a seahorse, dolphins, turtles or even a mermaid. Tape sweets onto the back to turn the game into a fun party activity.

Printing and Stamping

Printing and Stamping is a great way to create art – especially for kids who can't yet manage a brush to make pictures themselves. The great thing is that you need relatively little to get started and you can stamp very successfully using everyday objects.

Kids love to play with texture and shape, and they love anything that involves making a mess! The more freedom they have the more they'll enjoy it, so bear in mind that your child *will* get messy and paint *will* go everywhere. It's important that you're prepared beforehand – cover the table and anything else in the splatter zone and use a long-sleeved plastic bib for your child. Make sure the paint you're using is washable – not all child-friendly paint is.

Ideas for printing and stamping

Fruit and vegetable stamping
Cut a potato in half, then cut shapes into it from a paper template using a knife. You can also use cookie cutters to do this. Alternatively, rather than cutting a shape, the food can become the stamp – so go for interesting shapes: half an apple, cauliflower, peppers and lemons work well. For juicy fruits, squeeze a little first and dab to remove excess juice.

Bubble wrap
This makes a great textured print. Tape some onto a rolling pin before dipping it into paint and then transferring onto paper.

Balloons
These are wonderful for giant stamping. Pour some paint onto a large plate, dip in the balloons and turn the giant splodges into silly faces.

You will need

- Ready-mixed washable paint
- A variety of different-sized paintbrushes
- Sponges
- An old plate to put the paint on
- Things to stamp with (see opposite)
- Apron – for you as well as the kids
- Wipe-clean surface such as a plastic tablecloth
- Paper, card or fabric to stamp on

Corks and pencil erasers

These make perfect polka dots, or can be cut into with a knife to make shapes. Tie five pencils together, dip in paint and print to create sweet little flowers.

Leaves and flowers

These are great for stamping and kids can learn all about them. Leaves should be painted lightly to avoid splodges.

Hands, fingers and feet

Create some random stamps using hands and feet and then, once dry, turn them into funny creatures.

Masking-tape patterns

Apply strips of masking tape to a piece of paper. Paint over the top and then remove once dry to create a pattern.

Printing and stamping tips

Thicken paint: if the image is coming out a little runny, mix it with a bit of cornflour to thicken it up.

Make stationery: stamp on rolls of paper to turn your art into wrapping paper. Colours stand out well on brown paper. You could also print on cards and envelopes.

Decorate clothes: older children can use fabric paints to print on t-shirts, bags and so on.

Reuse: once you've used your potato stamp, wrap it in cling film and it will keep for a couple of days.

Get outside: stamping is a great outdoor activity, and it's easier to minimize mess out in the garden.

Build a Cardboard World

Create a nautical cardboard world with these three projects. Recycled boxes, tubes and cups are used to create a giant boat with an anchor and a retractable telescope. Children will learn how to build and construct objects and use imagination and logic to piece together their recycled treasure.

SKILLS LEARNED:
BUILDING AND CONSTRUCTION, PROBLEM SOLVING, MOTOR SKILLS, CUTTING AND STICKING, DRAWING AND COLOURING

Foldaway Cardboard Boat

This foldaway cardboard vessel comes complete with button control panel, flags and even an extending plank to send unruly pirates to the sharks. This boat is pretty large, but you could make it as big or small as you like. See also the Cardboard Anchor on page 42.

You will need

- Large cardboard box, 30 x 30 x 20in (76 x 76 x 50cm), for the boat

- 2 x pieces of 20 x 30in (66 x 76cm) corrugated cardboard, for the boat ends

- 6 x 60in (15 x 150cm) corrugated cardboard, for the plank

- 7 x 10in (18 x 25cm) corrugated cardboard, for the control panel

- 2 x pieces of 18 x 24in (46 x 60cm) corrugated cardboard, for the figurehead

- 4 x paper plates

- 6 x small bottle tops (twistable or capped) and 1 x large bottle top (from a detergent bottle)

- A roll of red, yellow and brown duct tape

- 3 x sheets of clear acetate or plastic, 8 x 12in (20 x 30cm)

- Blue acrylic paint and paintbrush

- Scissors

- PVA and strong glue

- Black felt-tip pen and a pencil

- 50in (130cm) length of 1in (2.5cm) dowelling

- Terracotta plant pot with a 1in (2.5cm) hole

- 3¼yd (3m) string

- 8 x 12in (20 x 30cm) sheets of card in the following colours: 1 x yellow, 2 x green, 2 x orange and 5 x red

- Scrap piece of card, approximately 4in (10cm) square

1 Open up the front and back of the square cardboard box by vertically cutting down two opposite corners. Open up the top flaps of the box so they stand up straight.

2 Take one of the 20 x 30in (66 x 76cm) pieces of cardboard and use coloured duct tape to attach it between the two cut open edges on one side of the box – overlapping each piece by 3in (8cm). This will create a pointed front to the boat. Repeat for the back and add tape along the matching sides for extra decoration. Cut off any flaps that are sticking out at the bottom of the boat.

3 Next, you need to cut some shape into the sides of the boat. In the centre of both long sides, measure and mark in pencil an 18in (46cm) line along the natural fold (for the top flaps). Then, from each end of the line, draw a diagonal line towards the top, going about a third of the way along the front piece of cardboard. Use scissors to cut this shape out.

4 Create a decorative figurehead for the boat by drawing a simple design onto cardboard. The design needs to measure around 22in (56cm) high with a straight edge to fit the front of the boat. Add a 3in (8cm) strip to the lower straight edge to create a tab to stick to the boat. Draw and cut one first, then flip it and draw around it to create another. Score along the tab line then glue the pieces together with PVA glue, leaving the tabs unglued. Use duct tape to attach the figurehead onto one end of the boat – this will now be the front. Cut a star from yellow and red card and glue in place on the figurehead for extra decoration.

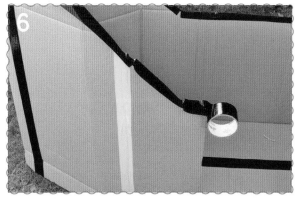

5 To create the door, mark the centre point of one side panel and measure 6in (15cm) either side of this point. Draw a line straight down on each side then cut down one of the lines and along the bottom.

6 Add duct tape along all the cut edges of the boat. Cut small tabs into the tape where it goes around bends and corners to keep the tape smooth.

7 Take a paper plate, cut off and discard the rim to make a template for the portholes. Place the template in the centre of one of the sides at the front, about 12in (30cm) from the top and draw around it, then cut

out. Repeat on the same side, towards the back of the boat. Make a third porthole using the paper plate in the door, 5in (12.5cm) from the top.

8 Take the remaining three paper plates and cut out the central circle, leaving the outer rim only. Paint the back of each one blue. Take the template used for the portholes and use it to measure and cut out three circles from acetate. Use strong glue to stick the acetate circles inside the plates. Add four black circles with black felt-tip pen to resemble bolts on the blue side of the plate. Glue them onto the three portholes you cut out from the boat, using strong glue.

Don't chuck out that box!

The cardboard measurements given should be used as a guideline rather than an exact requirement. Hang on to any big boxes or ask at an appliance store if they have any going spare.

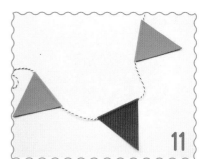

9 To make the plank, cut a 6 x 60in (15 x 150cm) piece of cardboard. Fold it into three equal pieces and add brown duct tape around the sides and on each fold. Tape it inside the bottom of the boat opposite the door, so that it can be folded out when the door is open.

10 To make the control panel, cut a piece of cardboard measuring 7 x 12in (18 x 30cm) and paint it blue. When the paint is dry, use strong glue to stick on six different bottle tops to create buttons and dials. Glue the panel inside the front of the boat.

11 Next, make bunting from green, red and orange card. Cut a 3in (8cm) triangle from a scrap of card to make a template. Fold a piece of coloured card in half, lengthways, and place the template onto the fold. Cut out six bunting flags from each colour. Lay out the string and glue inside the paper triangles. Stick the sides together, encasing the string along the top edge. Space the flags about 2in (5cm) apart.

12 Make a handle for the door by drawing around the large bottle top on the front of the door. Cut this out and insert the top, gluing at the back to secure in place.

13 For the flagpole, turn the plant pot upside down and insert the dowelling inside, taping it in place if you want extra stability. Place it in the centre of the boat. Tie the middle of the bunting around the top and place a little duct tape over the top to secure. Tie each end of the bunting to the front and back of the boat.

14 Make a 2in (5cm) slit in the back of the boat with scissors and attach the cardboard anchor from page 42.

Let's make!

This boat is just one idea for something that can be made from a cardboard box. Pretty much any play scene can be cut and taped together to create a cardboard world.

For a car: Place a rectangular box with the long side flat. Cut out a square in the middle of the top, keeping the front edge attached. Fold up and cut out the centre to create a windscreen. Cut doors on each side and add paper-plate wheels, then cut a flap in the back to create a boot.

For a theatre, shop or cafe: Place a rectangular box with the long side up. Cut out a square halfway up for the front, keeping the bottom edge attached. Fold this in half and tape down to create a ledge. Open up the back and add fabric for curtains and a cardboard sign on the top. Smaller boxes could be turned into mini household items like washing machines, TVs, cookers or a shop till. You could even turn a small toy suitcase into a dolls' house.

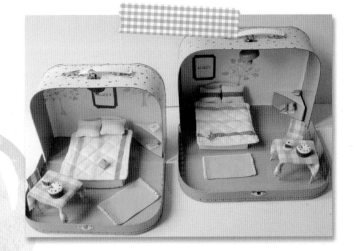

Let's play!

This boat makes a great centrepiece for a pirate-themed party. Add blue tarpaulin or old bedsheets around the boat with some grey cardboard shark fins tucked into the fabric. You can create an alternative to musical chairs using pillows for 'islands' - instead of stopping the music, an adult shouts 'Land ahoy!', and each child has to run from the boat to an island for safety. You could also put a small basket of plastic balls inside the boat for cannons and ask children to 'fire' them at the shark fins to knock them over.

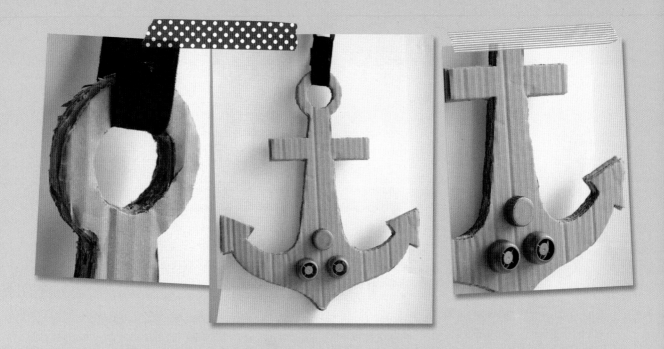

Cardboard Anchor

Land ahoy! This sturdy anchor can be fixed onto the cardboard boat (see page 36) and thrown overboard as soon as you reach dry land. Spray-painted bottle tops create a simple embellishment. Have a rummage through your recycling box to see what would work well, or add buttons, beads or even gems for a glitzy finish. Spray paint works really well for adding colour to plastic but bear in mind that this should be done by an adult in a well-ventilated area.

You will need

- 4 x pieces of corrugated cardboard, approximately 13 x 14in (33 x 36cm)

- 18 x 18in (46 x 46cm) square of black felt

- PVA glue

- Strong glue

- Scissors

- Pencil

- Copper acrylic spray paint

- 3 x bottle tops/small lids, 1in (2.5cm) in diameter

- Anchor template found on page 153

1 Photocopy the anchor template on page 153 and cut it out. Place it on top of the corrugated cardboard and draw around it in pencil four times. Cut out four anchors from the cardboard.

2 Glue the four cardboard anchor shapes together using PVA glue. Place a couple of heavy books on top of the anchor while drying so the layers stick together easily. When dry, trim away any bits that don't quite match up with scissors.

3 To make the chain, measure 1 x 7in (2.5 x 18cm) strips of black felt. Cut out 28 strips.

4 Fold over one strip of felt to form a circle. Overlap the ends by about ½in (1cm) and glue them together. Once dry, thread another strip through the first circle and fold to make another one. Glue and repeat until you have a chain that is about 70in (180cm) long. Leave two strips aside for attaching the chain to the anchor and the boat.

5 To attach the chain to the anchor, thread the final strip of black felt through the last circle on the chain and through the top of the anchor. Overlap the ends by about ½in (1cm) and glue together.

6 Lay a sheet of newspaper outside and place the bottle tops onto it. Spray paint them with copper paint and leave to dry. Glue these onto the front of the anchor at the bottom, using strong glue.

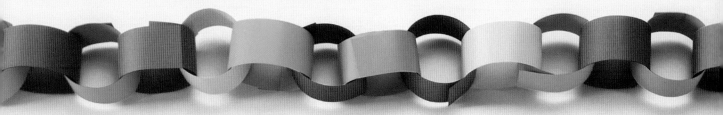

Let's make!

If you don't have any felt to hand to make the chain, you could use paper or card. Just bear in mind that it won't be quite as hardy in strong currents.

This method of layering card can be used to make other features for the boat. A steering wheel helm can be made by using a plate for a template, fixed to the bow using a strong elastic band threaded through the centre, like a button. You could also make oars, portholes, the ship's flag or even a giant sail.

Let's play!

Play a game of Anchor Toss, for two or more players. Make several circles from card using a dinner plate as a template and scatter them on the ground. Give each circle a different number, then place them on the floor (or around the Foldaway Cardboard Boat on page 36) with the low numbers nearest to you. Each shipmate has three attempts to throw the anchor onto the circles. The player with the highest score at the end wins. For younger players, use a hula hoop instead of circles for an easier target.

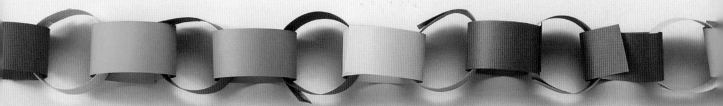

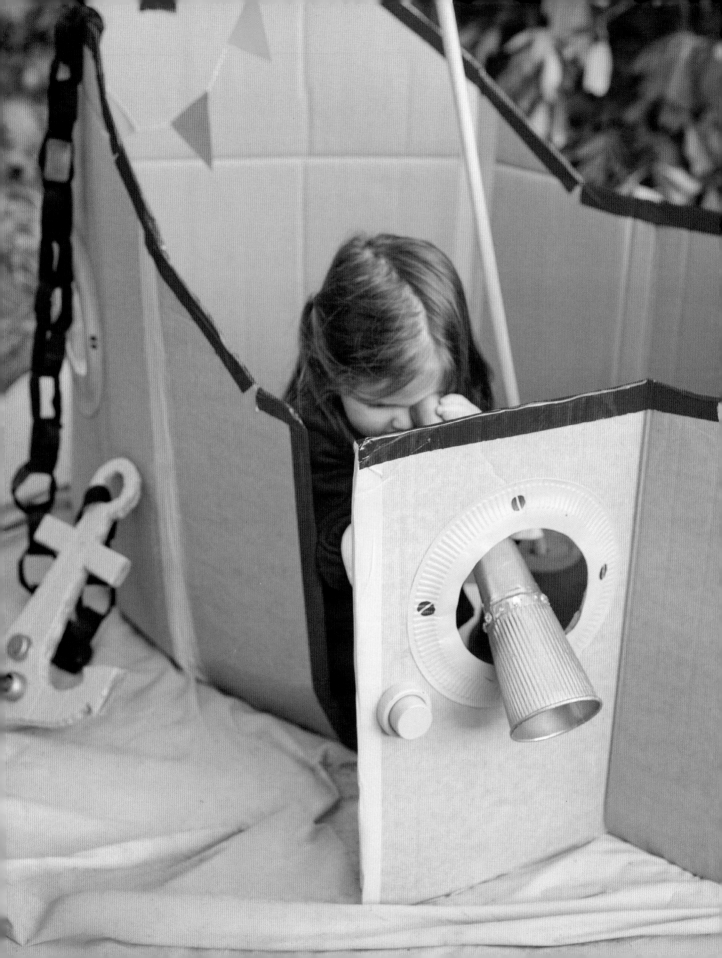

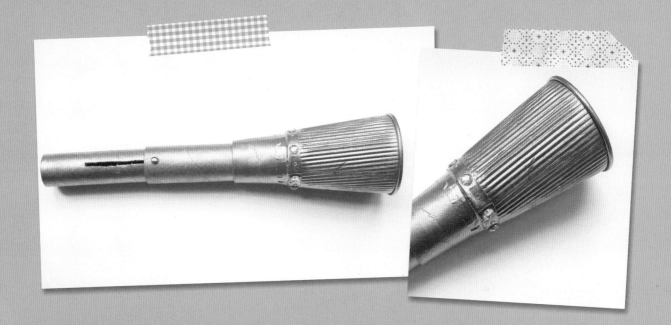

Retractable Telescope

This retractable cardboard telescope is the perfect accessory for any treasure-loving pirate. It is really easy to make from a couple of cardboard tubes and paper cups and even comes complete with its own nautical scene.

You will need

- 1 x cardboard tube, 5in (12.5cm) long

- 1 x cardboard tube, 4in (10cm) long

- 1 x small paper cup, 2¹/₂in (6cm) in diameter (an espresso-sized cup is ideal)

- 1 x larger paper cup, 3¹/₂in (9cm) in diameter (a standard coffee cup is ideal)

- Gold acrylic paint and paintbrush

- Duct tape

- Scissors

- 1 x paper fastener (split pin)

- 1 x plastic sheet or acetate, 3 x 3in (8 x 8cm)

- Coloured marker pens

- Craft knife

- Drawing pin

- Strong glue

- Mix of ¹/₂in (1cm) and ¹/₈in (2mm) glue-on gems (12 in total)

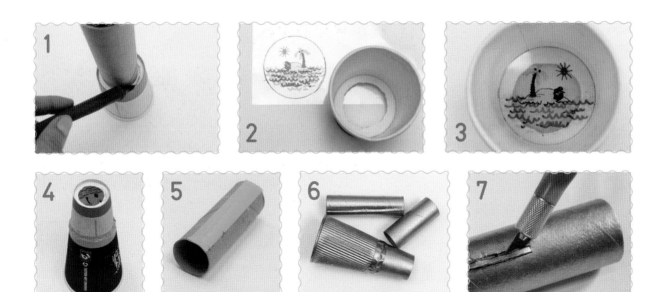

1 Begin by turning the small cup upside down and placing one of the cardboard tubes on top. Draw around the tube in pen. Use a craft knife to cut out the circle just inside the pen line so that the hole is a little smaller than the tube.

2 Turn the small cup the right way round and place it onto a piece of clear acetate or plastic. Draw around it with one of the marker pens, so that it doesn't smudge. Draw a nautical scene inside the circle using coloured marker pens. Keep it simple – a boat or a treasure island works well. Try to keep the main part of the image in the middle of the circle. If you want to be able to see through the telescope more easily, keep the scene to a little bit of wavy water at the bottom.

3 Cut out the plastic circle. On the inside of the cup, lightly glue all the way around the hole with strong glue. Stick your picture inside, being careful not to press it too hard to prevent any glue seeping out onto your picture.

4 Cut the bottom out of the big cup, using a craft knife. Use duct tape to attach the top of the little cup to the bottom of the big cup. You may need to snip the sides of the tape a little to prevent bumps.

5 Take a pair of scissors and cut the longer cardboard tube all the way along its length. Then press it back together with a ½in (1cm) overlap and tape all the way along the length with duct tape. Check it fits inside the smaller tube, if not, adjust the tape until it does.

6 Paint both tubes and cups gold. Paint the inside of the big cup too. Be careful not to get any paint on your nautical scene.

7 Measure a ⅛in (3mm) x 3in (8cm) slit on the long tube on the opposite side from the tape, ½in (1cm) from the bottom. Use a craft knife to carefully cut it out.

8 Poke a hole ½in (1cm) from the top of the short tube using a drawing pin, then push a paper fastener through the hole. Remove it and place the long tube inside the shorter one. Line up the slit on the long tube with the hole on the short tube. Push the paper fastener back through the hole and slit and fold it out loosely on the inside of the tubes. You should now be able to extend the longer tube up and down.

8

9

Let's play!

The telescope is a perfect accessory to the boat on page 36 and the anchor on page 42. Get dressed up and pretend you are looking for treasure. Making telescopes is a great party activity, just skip the extending part and stick to taping tubes to cups to keep it simple. Why not invite all your shipmates round and play a simple treasure hunt? Fill a shoebox decorated to look like a chest and hide it in your garden or house. Follow simple clues leading to a treasure map, which has an 'X' marking the spot of the treasure!

9 Use strong glue to attach the bottom of the short tube onto the stuck-together cups – be careful not to get glue on your picture. As a finishing touch, you can decorate the telescope by gluing gems onto the bottom of the large cup, spacing them roughly ½in (1cm) apart.

Let's make!

If you want to add some twinkly moveable waves to your seascape, add a strip of adhesive putty (such as Blu-Tack) around the edge of the acetate and pour in some blue sequins. Place another piece of acetate on top and glue into the cup.

Cardboard tubes and cups are brilliant for craft projects as you can stick, squash and glue them into different shapes. You can make a rocket by sticking two tubes together and adding a cup at the end. Paint the whole thing silver and add tissue paper fire and embellishments. You could also make mini party piñatas out of cardboard tubes decorated as bats, butterflies and bees. Add sweets to the bottom and seal it with a card base.

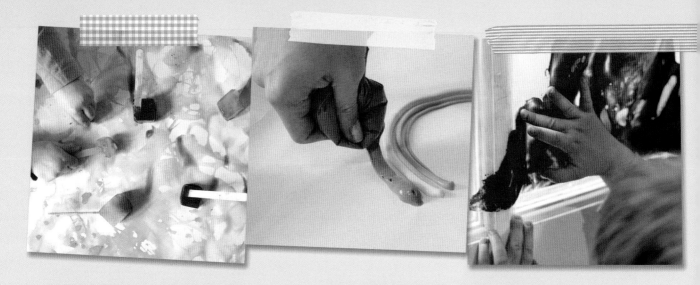

Painting and Drawing

Painting and drawing are fantastic activities to help children express themselves. They allow them to practice creating meaningful shapes and are a great way to develop coordination. Encouraging children to mix their paints will help them learn how colours blend together. Drawing is a nice mess-free alternative to painting and is a great introduction to handling a pen in preparation for learning to write.

You will need

Painting

- A selection of paints: watercolours, block paints, powder paints, puffy (see opposite) and glitter paint

- Things to paint with: paintbrushes, sponges and even pompoms make good dabbers when attached to a clothes peg

- Things to paint on: paper and card, but also canvas, fabrics and even outdoor walls if you're feeling brave!

- A long-sleeved apron

- Wipe-clean surface

- An easel with paint pots and a paper roll is a great idea if your kids love painting

Drawing

- Things to draw with: colouring pens, pencil crayons, watercolour crayons, wax crayons, whiteboard pens and chalks

- Things to draw on: paper, card, chalk and whiteboards

Ideas for painting and drawing activities

Zip-lock bags

This is a great introduction to painting and it is mess free! Simply fill a sealable bag with a mixture of different-coloured paints, tape to a window and let the child squish the colours together with their hands.

Puffy paint

Use three cups of shaving foam, one cup of flour and one cup of PVA glue to create paint that gives a three-dimensional effect. Mix the ingredients together (but not too much or you'll lose puffiness!) and divide it between three bowls. Mix food colouring into each one, then spoon the mixture into zip-lock bags. Snip off the tip of the corner on the bags and pipe out your pictures onto paper. The paint will remain puffy once dry.

Ice painting

Put water and food colouring into an ice-cube tray and add a lollipop stick to each one. Freeze, then use outside on sheets of card to create a watercolour painting effect. This is a great sensory activity, particularly for babies and toddlers.

Butterfly painting

Fold a piece of paper in half and cut into a butterfly shape. Place blobs of paint along one half, fold, press and open to reveal a colourful butterfly.

Painting and drawing tips

Separate paints: fill several pots with different-coloured paints and provide a different brush for each one, to avoid ending up with a brown mush of all the colours.

Save pens: revive pens that have dried out by leaving them, with the nibs down, in a bowl of water for five minutes.

Leave to dry on a paper towel then you're ready to reuse. Bear in mind this only works with water-based pens (which most children's pens are).

Display work: children feel an enormous sense of pride seeing their art on the walls.

Blowing paint with straws

Place dollops of watered-down paint onto paper and use straws to blow the paint around the page.

Rain art

Draw scribbles and shapes with watercolour pencils onto paper, place on a tray then leave outside in the rain. Sit in a comfy window and watch as the weather creates a masterpiece.

Abstract shape work

Draw an abstract shape on a piece of paper and see if the child can turn it into a familiar object such as a flower, monster or robot.

Body silhouettes

Draw around little hands and feet then turn them into monsters, ballerinas or crazy creatures. You could also draw around the whole of your child's body on a large roll of paper.

Time to Get Crafty

These projects help children to establish a daily routine and understand the concept of time in really simple ways. The canvas clock will help children recognize the order of their day and the sticky-felt calendar helps establish knowledge of days of the week and the weather.

SKILLS LEARNED:
NUMBER AWARENESS, DEVELOPING ROUTINES,
UNDERSTANDING OF DATE AND TIME,
CUTTING AND STICKING, PAINTING,
DRAWING AND COLOURING

Canvas Picture Clock

This project gives children a gentle introduction to telling the time and creates a visual timetable of the day – great for kids who are learning about numbers, time and daily routines. The clock is made from an art canvas and a clock mechanism. It has removable pictures depicting activities associated with different times of day. Build up your picture collection as your habits and routines change.

You will need

- Art canvas, 12in (30cm) square

- Dinner plate, approximately 10in (25cm) in diameter

- Clock mechanism (these are inexpensive and easy to buy online)

- Pencil

- Ruler

- Tape measure

- Acrylic paint in six different colours

- 12 x hook-and-loop dots, ½in (1cm) in diameter

- Stick-on numbers 1–12, ½in (1cm) high

- 1 or 2 sheets of A4 white card

- Felt-tip pens

- Circular lid, about 1½in (4cm) in diameter

- Paintbrush

- Scissors

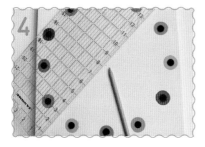  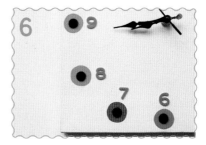

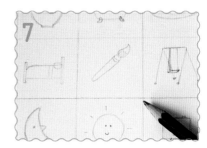

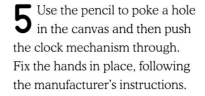

1 Find a dinner plate that is a little smaller than your canvas. Place it in the centre of the canvas and draw around it lightly with a pencil. Divide the circle into 12 equal parts and mark in pencil each of these points.

2 Find a circular lid about 1½in (4cm) in diameter – preferably translucent so that you can see the pencil marks underneath. Place it over each of the 12 marks on the circle and draw around it in pencil.

3 Paint each circle with brightly coloured acrylic paint. This may take a couple of coats for an even coverage.

4 Once the paint is dry, add a hook-and-loop dot to the centre of each circle. Using a tape measure, find the centre point of the canvas and mark it with a pencil.

5 Use the pencil to poke a hole in the canvas and then push the clock mechanism through. Fix the hands in place, following the manufacturer's instructions.

6 Take the stick-on numbers and attach them onto the clock next to each circle.

7 For the stick-on activities, use a pencil and ruler to draw out a grid with square boxes measuring 1½in (4cm) onto white card. Draw pictures in each square to represent a daily activity. Draw as many as you like, but bear in mind it is best if you have at least 12. Variations for different days would make the activity more engaging.

8 Colour in the pictures with bright felt-tip pens. Cut out the squares and then attach the opposite hook-and-loop dots onto the reverse of each picture.

Let's play!

Picture ideas

Day: sun, clouds or rain
Night: moon and stars
Mealtimes: breakfast,
lunch and dinner
Snacks: apples, bananas
Bathing: towel, soap
Bedtime: bed, toothbrush
Hobbies: paintbrushes,
pens and pencils
Playtime: teddies, dolls,
cars, TV and books
Games: dominoes, cards
and puzzles
Places: school, shop,
playgroup, swing, slide,
seesaw, bucket and spade

Children thrive on routine and love to know what they will be doing during the day. Filling up the clock with pictures of the day's activities could become a nice morning or bedtime ritual. You could also attach the activities to the clock as you are about to do them to encourage children to learn about the hours of the day.

Turn your clock into a game by placing all the activities face down, selecting them at random and then putting them on the clock at the correct times of day.

A fun way to learn and practise telling the time is for children to pretend to actually be clocks! Using their arms for the hands of a clock, pointing to the time is a good way to remember the location of the numbers and recognize the layout of a clock.

Let's make!

If you want to focus on telling the time rather than routine, replace the images on the cards with numbers that children can draw and colour themselves. You could also paint the hour and minute hand of the clock with acrylic paint to help children recognize the difference between each when learning to tell the time. Finally, for a more hands-on method, you can replace and interchange the clock mechanism with some cardboard hands (attached with a paper fastener) that can be moved to different times.

Clock mechanisms are surprisingly affordable, which means you can create a clock from anything you can punch a hole in! Paper plates, blackboards and fabric-covered embroidery hoops would all make interesting DIY clocks.

Sticky-felt Hanging Calendar

This felt calendar is the perfect way to introduce little ones to days of the week and the weather. Children can draw their own weather symbols for the calendar, or use the templates on page 152. When finished, it can be hung in an accessible place for little hands to change the pictures daily. Use this alongside the Canvas Picture Clock on page 56 and children will have days and routines sorted in no time!

You will need

- 1 x sheet of green felt, 6 x 11in (15 x 28cm)

- 1 x sheet of pale blue felt, 11 x 18in (28 x 46cm)

- A4 sheets of white, blue, light and dark yellow, brown, grey, orange and red felt

- White sewing thread and needle, or sewing machine

- Mixed pack of 1in (2.5cm) felt letters

- 14in (35cm) length of dowelling, ³/₄in (2cm) in diameter

- 30in (76cm) yarn

- Strong glue

- Tailor's chalk

- Ruler and pencil

- Pins

- Plain paper and scissors

- Weather symbol templates, found on page 152

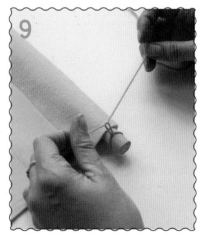

1 Begin by marking out the pockets on the piece of green felt. Turn the felt so it is in landscape layout. Measure 4in (10cm) from the left edge and draw a vertical line down the felt with tailor's chalk. Repeat from the right side to divide the felt into three segments (the middle one will be smaller).

2 Place the piece of blue felt in portrait layout and pin the green felt horizontally onto the lower section, aligning the bottom edges.

3 With a ¼in (6mm) seam allowance, sew all the way down the long edges of the blue felt, sewing over the green piece to attach them together. Then on the green felt, sew along the lines marked with tailor's chalk to create three pockets.

4 To make the house, cut out a 3in (8cm) square of red felt and a triangle from orange felt that measures 3 x 2 x 2in (8 x 5 x 5cm). Pin the square onto the blue section so that it just slightly overlaps the green felt in the centre. Sew ⅛in (2mm) from the edge, along the bottom and sides of the square.

5 Pin the orange triangle at the top of the square so that it slightly overlaps it and sew around, ⅛in (2mm) from the edge.

6 To make the channel for the dowelling, fold the top of the blue felt over towards the back by 2in (5cm). Pin it and sew ¼in (6mm) from the edge. Turn the bottom over towards the back by 1in (2.5cm) and sew in the same way.

7 On a piece of plain paper, draw out silhouettes for different types of weather (such as a cloud, sun, thunder and so on). These will form the templates for the felt, which will be stored in one of the pockets, so make sure they are smaller than the pockets. If you need inspiration, you can use the templates on page 152. Pin them to the different coloured felt and cut out.

8 Cut the red felt into seven more 3in (8cm) squares. Glue felt letters onto each square to represent the days of the week.

9 Insert the piece of dowelling into the channel at the top of the calendar. Cut the length of yarn in half, tie it to each end of the dowel and add a little strong glue over the top to secure it in place. Tie the yarn together at the top in a bow.

Let's make!

Add a storytelling element to the calendar by cutting out a felt family. Children can use the family, house and weather to retell their day or make up their own adventures. They could even add simple felt activities (for example, a football, ballet shoe or book) or little felt figures to represent their family, friends and pets. Faces could also be added in different colours to represent different moods and emotions (such as happy, sad, angry or worried). The child can then select how they are feeling each day.

Rock 'n' Roll up Your Sleeves

Get the earplugs ready – it's going to be noisy when these craft projects are finished! Children can paint, cut and create their own band from the contents of your recycling bin. Then they can get drumming, shaking and moving with their band mates to their favourite tunes.

SKILLS LEARNED:
MUSICAL AWARENESS, RHYTHM, PAINTING,
STICKING AND CUTTING, PAPIER MÂCHÉ,
REDUCING WASTE AND UPCYCLING

Butter-tub Banjo

This tuneful banjo is made from a cardboard tube and plastic tub, easily sourced with a quick rummage through your recycling bin. We've used a round tub but any container of a similar size would work, just make sure that it is sturdy as the elastic puts it under pressure. Each string of the banjo is strung at different levels to give a different tone.

You will need

- Strong cardboard tube (the type found inside cling film or tin foil are ideal), 14in (36cm) long

- Round plastic tub, 7in (18cm) in diameter

- Permanent pen

- Craft knife

- Masking tape

- Newspaper

- PVA glue and water

- Turquoise acrylic paint

- Paintbrush

- Pencil and ruler

- Strong glue

- 1yd (1m) of yellow elastic, $\frac{1}{16}$in (2mm) wide

- Jar lid, $2\frac{1}{2}$in (6cm) in diameter

- Child's plastic needle

- 6 x black two-hole buttons, $1\frac{1}{2}$in (2cm) in diameter

- 6 x paperclips

- Sharp scissors

- Large needle or pin

1 Stuff the cardboard tube with newspaper to add strength. Place the end of the tube onto one side of the tub, with the tube touching the lip of the lid. Draw around it with permanent pen, then use a craft knife to cut out and remove the circle from the tub.

2 Cut ½in (1cm) tabs into one end of the tube, about ¼in (6mm) apart. Remove the lid from the plastic tub and insert the end of the tube with the tabs through the hole in the tub. Tape down the tabs on the inside with masking tape.

3 Use the permanent pen to draw around the jar lid in the centre of the tub's lid. Cut out the circle.

4 To make the papier mâché, tear up the newspaper into small squares. Dip the pieces of paper into the glue and water mixture and cover the tub and tube with a layer of them, leaving the end of the tube (the one not attached to the tub) open. Do the lid separately, making sure not to cover the lip of the lid or the tub, so that you can put them back together afterwards. Finally, paint a layer of glue over the newspaper. Leave it to dry overnight and then repeat with a second layer, making sure there are no gaps between the pieces of newspaper. Leave to dry overnight.

5 Paint the outside of the banjo with turquoise acrylic paint and leave it to dry. You may need to do a few coats of paint for an even coverage.

6 Mark out the position of the holes on the cardboard tube with a pencil and ruler. Measure and mark ½in (1cm) down from the top of the tube and about ½in (1cm) to the right of the centre. Then measure ½in (1cm) to the left of the first mark and another ½in (1cm) down the tube (so 1in/2.5cm from the top altogether). Mark this point in pencil. Repeat this, starting from the second mark so that you have four marks in total.

7 To mark the position of the holes on the tub, draw a straight line ½in (1cm) below the cut-out circle on the lid (on the side of the tub without the cardboard tube attached). Then draw two vertical lines from the edges of the circle to the line (to allow you to find the centre). Measure and mark four points in pencil, each ½in (1cm) apart – make sure they are lined up centrally with the cut-out circle.

8 Use a pin to make holes in all the marks on the tube and the tub, then widen them with some sharp scissors.

9 Tie a double knot in the end of the length of elastic and thread it onto a plastic needle. Push it through the right-hand hole at the top of the tube, from the back. Remove the lid from the tub and thread the needle into the right-hand hole, from the front. Place the lid onto the tube, face up, and pull the elastic straight – but not taut. This will allow you to thread the strings on easily and when you replace the lid onto the tub, the elastic will be stretched taut. Come back in through the next hole in the lid, from the back, and through the corresponding hole on the tube, from the front. Continue to work across all the holes. Knot the elastic inside the last hole and cut away the excess. Place a line of strong glue inside the lip of the lid then stretch it down back onto the tub. Place a heavy book on top overnight, or until it has set.

Working with papier mâché

Papier mâché is a fun, but messy, craft so begin by covering your table with a wipe-clean tablecloth. To make the paste, mix two parts of PVA glue to one part water. It should be the consistency of double cream. Tear up the newspaper into small squares or strips. Torn edges work better than cut edges for achieving a smooth finish. Dip the strips into the paste and apply them to the surface. Cover the whole surface with paper, making sure there are no gaps. Use your fingers, or a clean paintbrush, to smooth out any creases and bubbles in the paper. Leave each layer to dry completely overnight. The more layers you add, the stronger the finished product will be.

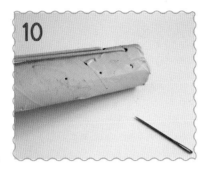

10 For the tuning pegs, use a large needle or pin to pierce a hole ½in (1cm) from the top of the tube, ½in (1cm) to the right of the top string hole. Pierce another 1in (2.5cm) below it, then another 1in (2.5cm) from that. Repeat on the other side.

11 Open up a paperclip so that it only has one bend. Cut the ends so that they are the same length then slide them through both holes in a button. Twist the wire and press the button flat. Do this six times.

12 Insert each paperclip and button into each of the holes and open out the wires inside the tube to secure. Stuff a little newspaper into the end of the tube to hold the wire in place, then cover the end with masking tape and paint on a little more turquoise paint.

Let's make!

Make a mini banjo for a doll or teddy by using a wide lollipop stick and a small circular cheese container. Cut in the same way and tape on rubber bands for the strings. Stringed instruments can be made from many things. You could make a shoebox guitar with its own cardboard plectrum or a paper-plate ukulele. If you want a realistic guitar, you could use several layers of corrugated cardboard cut to shape and stuck together (see the anchor on page 44 for the method) and use elastic or rubber bands for strings.

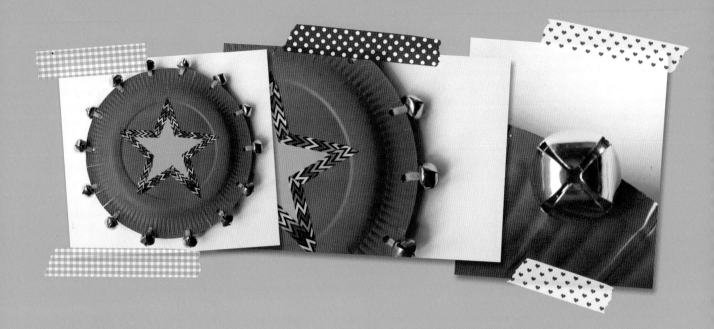

Paper-plate Tambourine

No rock band is complete without some percussion, and this funky paper-plate tambourine is a perfect project for mini makers to personalize and decorate. Bells make a great jingle, but you could also try metal bottle caps if you want a louder instrument. With your band behind you, all you need to do is start shaking.

You will need

- 2 x paper plates, 9in (23cm) in diameter
- Bright acrylic pink paint
- Paintbrush
- Approximately 3¹/₄yd (3m) of yarn
- Sewing needle
- 14 x ¹/₂in (1cm) bells
- 1 x sheet of yellow card, 8 x 12in (20 x 30cm)

- Roll of decorative tape, ³/₄in (2cm) wide
- Hole punch
- Pencil
- Ruler
- Scissors
- Star template, found on page 156

1 Begin by painting the back of the plates with bright paint and leave them to dry completely. You may need to do a few coats to cover the plates evenly.

2 Next, mark out the holes for the bells. Put a ruler along the edge of the front of one of the plates, measure and mark at 2in (5cm) intervals in pencil. Continue all around the plate. From each mark, measure ½in (1cm) down the plate and punch holes at these points all the way round. Repeat this for the other plate.

3 Photocopy and cut out the star template on page 156 and draw around it to create two stars on yellow card. Cut them out and glue them centrally onto the back of each plate.

4 Cut a 2½in (6cm) strip of decorative tape, then cut it in half lengthways. Place the pieces along one edge of the star, then cut more pieces and continue all the way around both stars to add a funky decoration.

5 Place the plates together with the starred sides facing out. Line up the holes around the edges so that they match, then sew on the bells with yarn. Tie a knot in one end of the yarn, thread on a bell and feed it through a hole. Sew through the hole about five times and secure with a knot at the back. Cut off any excess yarn. Repeat all the way around the plate.

Let's make!

The basic principle of two paper plates glued together can form a few other percussion instruments too. Glue the plates together and fill with dried pulses, rice or beads to create shakers. Each filling will produce a different sound. Cut a hole in one of the plates, pierce small holes and thread rubber bands on before gluing the plates to create a simple stringed instrument. If you want to save time, use coloured paper plates so you don't have to paint them first!

Let's play!

Tambourines and other percussion instruments are a great introduction to musical rhythm and beat. Explore the different ways to produce sounds with your tambourine - shaking, tapping like a drum or hitting against your hands and knees. Make some noise by playing Shake and Stop! Turn on your favourite tunes and shake or tap the tambourines as loudly as you can along to the beat. Pause the music suddenly for everyone to stop and freeze in a silly pose. You can play this game with the other instruments in this book too and any other noisy bells, rattles and maracas you can find.

Recycled Drum Kit

This drum kit is made from reused tins, tubs and lids and is a fantastic way to make something great from rubbish. Have a rummage through your recycling and select the pots, tins and lids that you'd like to use. Large tins for paint or formula milk are great for drums, and yogurt pots or soft cheese tubs add different tones to the kit. Give them a little tap with a chopstick to see what they sound like before shortlisting them for your kit! The drums are covered in masking tape, which is then removed to create a relief effect when painted.

You will need

- A selection of old tins, tubs, pots and lids, thoroughly cleaned and labels removed

- 2 x balloons

- Acrylic spray paint in silver, blue, green, pink and white

- About 10 x 20in (25 x 50cm) corrugated cardboard

- Strong glue

- Hammer and a nail

- Decorative duct tape, ³/₄in (2cm) wide

- Masking tape

- 5 x wooden chopsticks (or similar-sized pieces of dowelling)

- Vice

- Pencil and scissors

1 Be careful with sharp edges when opening and using the tins. You can sand these down with a metal file if necessary. Lay all the tins, tubs, pots and lids out to get an idea of how you might arrange them. Test the sound with a tap of a chopstick.

For this kit, we've used:
1 x large paint tin
2 x small tins
1 x small tub
1 x large tub
1 x jam-jar lid
1 x larger plastic lid

2 Put the small tins to one side then paint the large tin and both tubs white, and the lids silver. Spray paint is best for this as it will stick to the metal and plastic on the pots well. Leave them to dry completely. Next, create patterns on the drums using masking tape in any shape you like. Vertical strips of tape will make stripes, vertical and horizontal ones for squares or diagonal strips to create triangles.

3 Spray paint the tins different colours and leave to dry once more. Put the large tin open side up before spray painting so that the bottom doesn't get any paint on it – this will become the skin of your drum. When they are dry, peel away the masking tape to reveal your pattern.

4 For the skins on the two smaller tins, cut a balloon in half across the width and discard the tube end. Stretch the balloons over the open side of the tin, then wrap a strip of decorative duct tape around the sides to secure.

5 To make the cymbal, use the silver jam-jar lid. Put a little decorative tape around the wide end of a chopstick and place it into a vice, tape side up. Use a hammer to carefully nail the lid onto the chopstick. If you don't have a vice, you could also glue the chopstick to the end of the dowel using extra-strong glue. Bear in mind that it may not

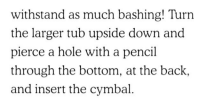

withstand as much bashing! Turn the larger tub upside down and pierce a hole with a pencil through the bottom, at the back, and insert the cymbal.

6 Place a chopstick onto the side of one of the smaller tins, with the wide end aligning with the bottom of the tin and tape in place. Repeat for the other tin.

7 Use more duct tape to attach the chopsticks onto the back of the larger tin so that one is slightly higher than the other.

8 Arrange the drum kit on top of a piece of cardboard. Draw around the outline of the tins. Cut out the shape on the cardboard, paint it blue and use strong glue to stick the drum-kit pieces onto it.

9 For the drumsticks, add decorative tape to the top of each remaining chopstick.

Let's play!

Playing a beat game with children is a good way for them to learn about rhythm and improve their memory. Tap out a simple beat on the drum kit for your child to copy. Start with only two taps and add another beat each time – see how many you can both get to. You could even add to the beat with a shake of a paper-plate tambourine (see page 72).

Let's make!

If your little ones love to make a noise, you could recycle an old cake tin and turn it into a marching drum. Clean and paint your tin and lid, then drill holes in either side. Attach a ribbon or cotton tape as a strap using a nut and bolt or rivets. Add dried pulses, lentils or rice into the tin and glue the lid on. You can either use chopsticks or pieces of dowel for the drumsticks.

Mini Microphone

Select your lead singer and add the final touch to your band with this super-easy microphone. Here we've used a styrofoam ball, but you could also use a foam tennis ball. The microphone features buttons and beads for switches and a handy keyring as the lead, which clips onto a pocket or belt loop to enable your mini maker to be ready to sing up a storm at the shake of a tambourine.

You will need

- 1 x 3in (8cm) styrofoam ball
- Black and silver acrylic paint
- Paintbrush
- 1 x cardboard tube, 4in (10cm) long
- 1 x green button, ½in (1cm) in diameter
- 1 x orange bead, ½in (1cm) in diameter
- Strong glue
- Decorative tape
- Black plastic spiral keychain
- Sharp scissors
- Masking tape

Let's make!

Want to add a little bit more bling to your microphone? Paint a thin layer of PVA glue onto the tube, sprinkle glitter liberally then add some sequins for a super-sparkly finish. You could also make mini microphones for your teddies – just cut the tube down a bit and make the cone a little smaller, then use a ping-pong or small styrofoam ball for the head. Cardboard tubes of all lengths are a great basis for many different crafts because they are so versatile. Build up a stash ready to be turned into telescopes (see page 47), monsters, racing cars or even swords. Perfect for a rainy-day boredom buster.

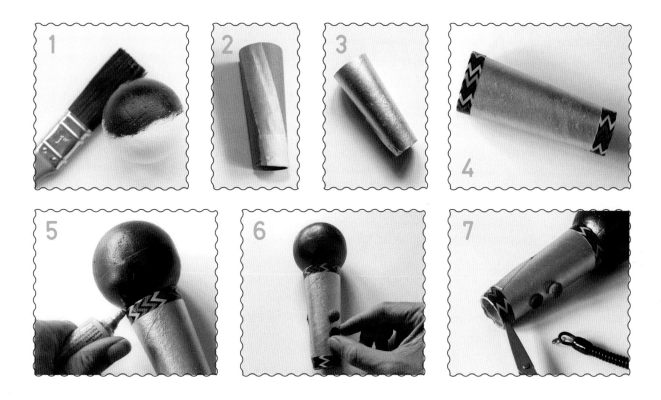

1 Paint the styrofoam ball with black acrylic paint.

2 Take the cardboard tube and cut all the way along the length. Take the cut sides and push them back together, overlapping by 1in (2.5cm) at the base to create a cone shape. Tape the cone shape together along the length with masking tape.

3 If there are any rough edges on either end of the tube, trim them with scissors so that the openings are smooth. Then paint the tube silver.

4 Stick the decorative tape around the top and bottom edges of the tube.

5 Put a line of the strong glue around the rim of the widest end of the cone and glue the ball on top. Then put another line of glue around the outside of the join to give it extra strength. Leave to dry completely.

6 Glue the button and bead onto the tube to create the 'on' and 'off' buttons. You could also use sequins, small bottle caps or small pompoms.

7 Finally, to attach the 'lead', pierce a hole ½in (1cm) from the bottom of the cone with a pair of sharp scissors and attach the plastic spiral with the keyring attachment. The other end can then be clipped onto belt loops ready to sing your heart out.

Cooking and Baking

Kids love cooking. It offers so much variety that it never needs to get boring. They can get involved with every aspect – from making their own meals, creating edible gifts, baking and decorating cakes and biscuits, to scraping out the bowl and washing up. Getting children involved in the kitchen is really important to help them understand where their food comes from, how dishes come together and how easy and fun it can be to make something yummy. Cooking is a brilliant way to introduce new foods and tastes to fussy eaters too – children are far more likely to eat something if they have helped to make it.

Cookery ideas
Pizza faces
Add tomato sauce and toppings to pizza bases, toast or French bread and arrange them to look like a face. This is a great way to try new vegetables.

Veggie omelettes
Prepare a mixture of finely chopped vegetables then get kids to crack the eggs, grate the cheese and add a splash of milk, before whisking up for you to cook.

You will need

- An apron (make sure jumper sleeves are rolled up out of the way)

- Ingredients (laid out for ease)

- A low, wipe-clean surface, such as an oilcloth or plastic tablecloth

- Basic cookery equipment

Safety in the kitchen

Take extra care with children in the kitchen with sharp and hot things around. Use blunt knives, keep little hands away from hobs and oven doors and make sure pan handles aren't within reach.

Sandwich spirals

Cut the crusts off two pieces of bread and lay them on a chopping board with the ends overlapped. Then use a rolling pin to flatten them, add your fillings and roll up like a Swiss roll. Cut and serve.

Fruit kebabs

Let kids load their chopped-up favourite fruits onto a wooden skewer. These can even be dipped in Greek yogurt and frozen on hot days.

Rocky road

Put digestive biscuits in a plastic bag and bash with a rolling pin. Mix with marshmallows, raisins and other dried fruits, then mix in melted chocolate. Press into a baking tin and place in the fridge to harden.

Pancakes

Kids can help whisk up a cup of flour, a cup of milk and an egg to make the pancake batter. Once an adult has cooked the pancakes in a frying pan with a little butter, let the kids fill them with chopped bananas, chocolate spread, blueberries and yogurt before rolling them up and devouring.

Smoothies

Chuck fruit and vegetables with some yogurt and fruit juice into a blender and watch as it whizzes them up into wonderful colours. From pink and pretty strawberry smoothies to green mixtures with added spinach, this is a great way to eat healthily.

Cooking and baking tips

Avoid squabbles: if you're planning on cooking with more than one child, make sure each child has their own bowl and spoon and get them to mix their own portion, combining what they've made before it goes in the oven. Or, give them different jobs – one weighing the ingredients while the other mixes them together.

Be prepared: although cooking can be a great spur-of-the moment rainy-day activity, if you're not prepared, it can quickly turn messy. Having a clear idea about what you are going to make, reading the recipe beforehand, covering surfaces and laying the ingredients out will help.

Teddy Bears' Picnic

These projects will provide your little crafter with everything needed to throw a picnic for their teddies and friends. The tea set is a great way to practise using air-dry clay; the teddy biscuits are easy to make, fun to decorate and taste yummy and they can all be stored in the clever cake tin.

SKILLS LEARNED:
BAKING, SHARING, MOULDING CLAY, PAINTING, CUTTING AND STICKING

Clay Tea Set

This lovely play tea set is made from air-dry clay, which has a very similar consistency to regular clay, but does not need to be fired. This makes it a great, inexpensive material for kids' crafts. Bear in mind that it is not as strong as normal clay, so keep the pieces thick for extra strength. This type of clay isn't waterproof either, so make sure any 'tea' going into the cups is pretend! The pieces (particularly the teapot) will need to dry between each stage of making, so you will need to do this project over several days.

You will need

- Approximately 1lb 10$\frac{1}{2}$oz (750g) air-dry clay
- Small china teacup
- Small bowl, about 5in (12.5cm) in diameter
- Scissors
- Yellow and blue acrylic paint
- Fine paintbrush
- Cling film
- Cookie cutter, 3$\frac{1}{2}$in (9cm) in diameter
- Cookie cutter, 1$\frac{1}{2}$in (4cm) in diameter
- Rolling pin
- Knife
- Emery board or sandpaper
- Strong glue
- Pencil
- Craft varnish (optional)
- Teapot template, found on page 153

Working with air-dry clay

Make sure you have a clean plate or tray to work on and keep a small cup of water to hand to smooth cracks or join pieces together. Break off the amount of clay needed and put the rest into cling film to stop it drying out. If it does start to crack and dry a little, dip it in the water and work it in your hands until it is soft and malleable again. It is useful to roll out the clay on the cling film too so that you can pick it up, move it and check the thickness. The clay will need to dry overnight before it can be painted. It will dry quicker in a warm place, so sit it in a sunny spot by a window or in an airing cupboard to dry out. If there are any rough edges on the dry clay these can easily be sanded with fine sandpaper or an emery board.

1 To make a clay cup, start by lining the inside of a small china teacup with cling film. Take a golf ball-sized lump of air-dry clay and press it out into a circle, about 4in (10cm) wide and ½in (1cm) thick. Press this circle into the teacup and push it gently down so that it sits nicely against the base and walls of the cup.

2 Use the cling film to pull the clay carefully out of the cup. Use a pair of scissors to cut away the rough edges around the top of the cup to make it even. The clay cup should be about 1½in (4cm) tall.

3 Place the cling film and clay back into the cup. Dip your finger into a little water and smooth the insides of the clay to remove any lumps or wrinkles. Pull the clay out again, remove the cling film and leave to dry. As the clay is quite thick, it may take a couple of days to harden. Repeat Steps 1–3 to make a second cup.

4 Once the cups are dry, you can sand any rough edges with an emery board or sandpaper to make them smooth. To make the handles, roll clay sausages that measure ¼ x 2in (6mm x 5cm). Bend them into a 'C' shape and press one end, curled under, against the side of the cup (it does not need to stick). Press the other end, uncurled at the base. Remove and set aside to dry, then glue in place.

5 To make a saucer, roll out another golf ball-sized lump of clay onto some cling film until it is about ¼in (6mm) thick. Use the large cookie cutter to cut a circle from the clay.

6 Use the cling film to lift the circle and place it into a small bowl (it should be about 5in/12.5cm wide at the top – you want the edges of the clay to just bend up a little around the base of the bowl to create the lip of the saucer). Press the circle into the base of the bowl and smooth down the edges with a little water.

7 Take the small cookie cutter and press lightly into the centre of the clay to create an indentation. Be careful not to go too deep as it will weaken the clay when dry. Remove the clay from the bowl with the cling film and leave in a warm place to dry (if the clay is very soft, leave it in the bowl to set for a bit first). Repeat Steps 5–7 to make a second saucer.

8 To make a teapot, photocopy and cut out the teapot template found on page 153. Roll out 5¼oz (150g) of clay to about ¼in (6mm) thick. Place the template on top of the clay and cut out two pieces. Smooth the tops with your fingers and a little water.

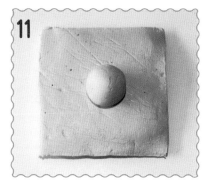

9 For the teapot sides, roll out another golf ball-sized lump of clay to ¼in (6mm) thick and cut out two rectangles that measure 3 x 2in (8 x 5cm). Take one rectangle and press it along the edge of one of the teapot pieces, along the inside. Pinch and smooth it in place. Take the other rectangle and do the same on the other edge of the same piece. Then take the other teapot piece and place it onto the other side, pinching and smoothing in place. Leave in a warm place until it is relatively sturdy before starting the next step.

10 Roll out 2½in (6cm) ball of clay on a piece of cling film to ¼in (6mm) thick. To create the base, place the teapot on top and cut around it with a knife. Gently turn the teapot upside down and place the cut-out piece of clay on top. Smooth the pieces together so that there are no gaps.

11 With the teapot still upside down, make the lid from the same piece of rolled-out clay. Cut around the top of the teapot to create a square. Then cut out another square ½in (1cm) smaller than this piece and press it in the centre of the larger piece. Turn it around and roll a cherry-sized piece of clay into a ball and press this gently on top – it does not need to stick at this stage. Leave to dry.

12 To make the spout, roll out a cocktail sausage-sized piece of clay. Press it against the side of the teapot and push and squash it so that it angles upwards like a spout. Remove and push the end of a pencil into the end to look like a hole. For the handle, take another piece of clay the same size, but roll it out to 4in (10cm) long. Fold into a 'C' shape, as for the teacup handle, then remove both pieces and leave to dry. Glue in place onto the teapot.

13 Finally, all you need to do is decorate the tea set using acrylic paint. Mark out your patterns with pencil, then fill in with the paint and a fine brush. If you want added shine and strength, add a coat of craft varnish once the paint is dry.

Let's play!

Bring out your teddies, lay out a nice rug and set out your lovely new tea set for a perfect garden picnic. Encourage kids to use their imaginations and collect things from around the garden to use in their 'picnic' – leaves for biscuits, twigs for teaspoons, pebble sugar lumps and delicate daisy sweeties. You can even bring out the magnetic cake from page 96 to add to the picnic.

Let's make!

You could also make a more basic tea set from salt dough (see the recipe on page 146), but test a small area first if you are varnishing, as some varnishes don't react well with the dough. You could also make and paint clay versions of your favourite cookies to go with your tea set. Cut them out using cookie cutters and sandwich the dry pieces together using wet clay, to create a cream-filled effect. If you want to add to the set, make yourself a dainty sugar pot, milk jug and teaspoons.

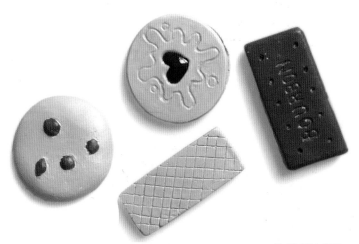

Magnetic Cake

Create a play cake from a metal biscuit tin using paint, clay and magnets. Kids will love moulding and painting their favourite toppings for the cake. You can make anything you like to top your cake as long as the base is flat so that you can attach a magnet. The tin also makes a handy storage place for the toppings or other edible treats. Allow a couple of days to give time for the toppings to dry.

You will need

- Metal biscuit tin (this one measures 7¹/₂in/19.5cm in diameter)

- Acrylic paint: brown, white and red for the cake and a variety of other colours for the decorations

- Regular and fine paintbrushes

- 3¹/₂oz (100g) air-dry clay

- Mini letter or number cutters (optional)

- Craft varnish

- 1 x magnetic sheet, 4 x 4in (10 x 10cm) square

- 1 x sheet of white paper, 8 x 12in (20 x 30cm)

- Felt-tip pens

- Double-sided tape

- Sticky tape

- 5 x cocktail sticks

- Scraps of orange and yellow card

- Strong glue

- Sharp pencil

- Scissors

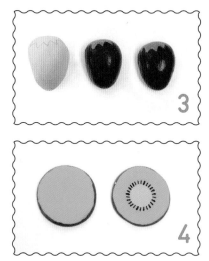

1 Begin by giving the cake tin a good clean to ensure the paint will stick to the surface. If there is any oil or grease, the paint will bubble. Once it is completely dry, keep the lid separate and paint the base of the tin brown and the lid white. Then paint a wobbly white line to look like cream around the middle of the base, about ¼in (6mm) wide. Paint another thin red line along the centre of the white one for the jam filling.

2 Use the edge of a fine brush to paint little sprinkles (roughly ¼in/6mm long) in pastel colours on the top of the cake.

3 To make the strawberries, take a 1½in (4cm) ball of air-dry clay and press it onto the plate to create a flat side. Pinch one end to make it narrower. Once dry, mark a zigzag line in pencil across the top, near the wider end for the stalk. Paint red and green, then add black seeds with a fine brush.

4 To make the kiwi fruit, roll out the clay to a thickness of ¼in (6mm). Use a 1½in (4cm) cutter (or cut around a lid that is roughly this size) to cut out circles from the clay. Once dry, paint the fronts green and the edges brown. Add a pale green circle in the centre, then add black seeds around the circle with a fine brush.

5

7

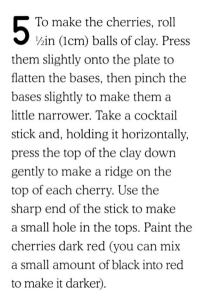

6

9

8

10

5 To make the cherries, roll ½in (1cm) balls of clay. Press them slightly onto the plate to flatten the bases, then pinch the bases slightly to make them a little narrower. Take a cocktail stick and, holding it horizontally, press the top of the clay down gently to make a ridge on the top of each cherry. Use the sharp end of the stick to make a small hole in the tops. Paint the cherries dark red (you can mix a small amount of black into red to make it darker).

6 For the chocolate drops, take a ½in (1cm) piece of clay, roll it into a ball and press down until it is about ¼in (6mm) in diameter. Smooth the edges with a little water so that they are nicely rounded. Paint brown.

7 To make the marshmallows, take a ½in (1cm) piece of clay and roll it into a ball. Pinch it between your finger and thumb, and with your other finger and thumb roll it back and forth to create a cylindrical shape. Paint pale pink or white.

8 To make the tangerine segments, roll a ¾in (2cm) lump of clay into a ball, then roll it into a sausage shape about 1¼in (3cm) long. Press to create a flat base and pinch the ends to taper them. Bend the clay so that it forms a curled shape. Paint the segments orange.

9 Roll out a piece of clay to a thickness of around ¼in (6mm) and cut out with letter cutters to spell names, messages or ages. If you don't have letter cutters, you could cut around printed letters with a knife. Paint any colour you like.

10 Once your toppings are painted and have dried, they can be varnished to give a glossy appearance and make them a little tougher.

11 To make the toppings magnetic, place them on top of the magnetic sheet and draw around them with a sharp pencil. Make sure you draw onto the non-magnetic side – test it out on your tin if you aren't sure. Cut around the pencil drawings just inside the lines so that the magnetic bases are slightly smaller than the toppings and therefore hidden. Glue the magnets onto the bottom of the toppings with strong glue.

12 To make the candles, take a piece of white paper and draw on four rectangles measuring 2½ x 6in (6.5 x 15cm). Fill each rectangle in with diagonal stripes using a felt-tip pen. Cut these out. On the reverse of the paper, place a strip of double-sided tape along each narrow end, and another down the middle. Peel away the back of the tape and place a cocktail stick at one end, with the bottom of the stick lined up with the

bottom of the paper. Carefully roll the paper around the stick. Trim off the tip of the cocktail stick with scissors so it isn't sharp. Wrap sticky tape around the candle to protect it.

13 For each candle, cut a small flame (about ¾in/2cm high) from orange card and a slightly smaller one from yellow card. Glue them onto the candle tops, with the wick sandwiched between them.

14 To make a candle base, take a ¾in (2cm) ball of air-dry clay. Push the end of the candle into it and twist around a little. Then, with the candle still in place, pinch the clay to make corners. Remove the candle and, once dry, paint purple. Follow Step 11 to attach the magnetic sheet to the bottom of the candles.

Let's play!

Make the magnetic cake the centre of your teddy bears' picnic. Lay a blanket on the floor and invite all your cuddly friends to the party. 'Light' the candles and sing happy birthday, then open the tin and enjoy some real tasty treats like the teddy bear biscuits found on page 102.

You can play with the cake too: why not arrange the toppings into shapes, faces, patterns or letters? Little ones can practice spelling out their names and counting with the letter and number magnets. You could also place the toppings inside the tin and ask friends to close their eyes, pick one and guess what it is. Or, share out the toppings and see who can place theirs nearest to the centre of the cake with eyes closed.

Let's make!

Use different sizes and shapes of tins to create a whole variety of yummies – like chocolate cake or fruity trifle. But why stop at cakes? A tin lid would make a great pizza: paint the edges brown and the centre red, with strips of yellow paper glued on for grated cheese. Make clay toppings such as pepperoni, pineapple, olives, mushrooms and ham. With a good selection, you could have a different pizza every time.

You could even flip the lid around, paint it to look like a plate and make some meal items – fried egg, sausage and toast for breakfast perhaps, or fruit and biscuits for dessert. Kids will love making funny combinations of foods to eat.

Teddy Bears' Picnic Cookies

These simple cookies are the perfect accompaniment to a teddy bears' picnic. Store them inside the magnetic cake tin (see page 96) and serve them up with a little cup of air from your lovely new tea set (see page 89). This cookie mixture can be made in minutes and it doesn't spread, making it ideal for cookie cutters and little hands. The royal icing uses egg whites, but you could use pasteurized egg-white powder if you prefer.

You will need

For the cookies (makes 8–10):

- 6oz (175g) plain flour
- A pinch of salt
- 6oz (75g) caster sugar
- 2oz (50g) ground almonds
- 5oz (150g) butter, at room temperature
- A few drops of almond essence
- Rolling pin
- Teddy-shaped cookie cutter
- Baking sheet
- Baking paper

For the icing:

- 1 egg white
- 1 teaspoon lemon juice
- 7oz (200g) icing sugar, sifted
- Food colouring in two or three colours
- 2 or 3 zip-lock bags
- Electric mixer (or balloon whisk)

To decorate:

- Hundreds and thousands
- Chocolate drops
- Small jelly sweets
- White and milk chocolate buttons and stars

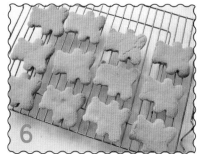
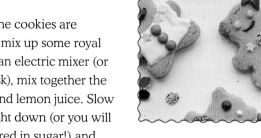

1 Preheat the oven to 350°F/180°C/Gas Mark 4. Mix together the dry ingredients in a bowl.

2 Add the almond essence and rub in the butter with your fingers. Kids love getting their hands stuck in! Try to encourage them to use their fingers rather than their whole hands to avoid warming the mixture.

3 Bring the mixture together with your hands and then roll out to a thickness of about ¼in (6mm) on a floured surface. Cut with the cookie cutter and place on a greased and lined baking sheet. Bake for 10–15 minutes, or until golden.

4 While the cookies are baking, mix up some royal icing. Using an electric mixer (or balloon whisk), mix together the egg whites and lemon juice. Slow the mixer right down (or you will end up covered in sugar!) and gradually add the icing sugar until you have a smooth paste.

5 Divide the mixture into two or three bowls and add a dab of food colouring to each. Mix until the colour is consistent. Spoon each colour carefully into a zip-lock bag, squeeze away the air and seal.

6 When the cookies are baked, place them onto a wire rack and leave them to cool completely.

7 Snip a tiny bit of the corner off each icing bag to create a piping bag. Kids can then let their imaginations run wild by decorating their teddies, giving them clothes, features or just colouring them in. Decorate the bears with jelly sweets for buttons, hundreds and thousands and chocolate drops, while the icing is still wet. Chocolate buttons can be cut in half to create ears, or use two quarters for a bow tie, or one quarter for a nose. Put the biscuits to one side to completely set, this will take about two hours.

Let's make!

Decorating biscuits is a great way to entertain kids on a rainy day. Icing can be made in advance and stored in zip-lock bags for up to a week in the fridge, so you can be ready to snip the bag and decorate at a moment's notice. For older children, using icing is a great way to practise writing. Encourage them to personalize larger biscuits with their initials.

Putting on a Show

This section will teach you how to make your very own personalized puppets from just a few basic supplies. Turn your family into flying, jumping paper puppets, ready to perform in their very own theatre. Encouraging children to take part in role play and perform helps build confidence.

SKILLS LEARNED:
LANGUAGE AND SOCIAL SKILLS,
CONFIDENCE, PERFORMANCE, PAINTING,
CUTTING AND STICKING

Dancing Family Puppets

Children will love making their family dance and act out silly scenes. Seeing them jig around and fling their legs and arms into oddly athletic poses will create endless giggles. Build the mini theatre on page 112 and host your own family spectacular. This project uses miniature paper fasteners, which are available in larger craft stores or online. You could also use regular-sized fasteners, but you might need to make your puppets a little bigger.

You will need

- Digital camera

- Access to a computer and colour printer

- 1 or 2 sheets of 8 x 12in (20 x 30cm) photographic paper

- Miniature paper fasteners/split pins (12 per puppet)

- Cardboard for backing, such as a cereal box

- Glue and scissors

- Large needle

- Adhesive putty (such as Blu-Tack)

- Lollipop sticks (three per puppet)

- Hammer

- 1in (2.5cm) nail

1 Begin by taking family photos with a digital camera. They will need to be full-length, forward-facing images. Ideally the subjects will have both feet on the ground and arms hanging to the sides (see box). Upload to a computer and scale the photos so that the adults are about 6in (15cm) high, with the children scaled smaller, around 4in (10cm) for a three-year-old. To get the right size, resize your photos and print out testers on normal paper. Print the final pictures onto photographic paper.

2 Roughly cut out around each person and then glue them onto the card. Cut each body into six separate segments: cut the arms and legs off the body, then cut the arm and leg pieces in half at the joints.

3 Now the puppets will need to be joined back together using the paper fasteners. Use a large needle and some adhesive putty to push holes into each limb and body piece just next to where the pieces have been cut.

4 Connect the joints of the puppets back together again, using the paper fasteners.

5 Arrange the arms and legs of the puppet so that they are pointing down, then place a lollipop stick under the left hand and foot, with the foot at the bottom of the stick. Push the needle through the foot and hand to mark the stick.

6 Take the nail and lightly hammer it into the marks to make holes.

Let's play!

Using the puppet theatre from page 112, you can put on an incredible family show – with dancing dads, majestic mums and fantastic flying kids. Hold the puppets from above to dance around the stage. Ask each family member to operate their own puppet and act out a scene.

Puppets make a great learning resource. They can be used to develop language skills by encouraging children to act out dialogues and practise the art of conversation. They can also be great for demonstrating behaviour, such as how to share toys or what to do when someone is unhappy by acting out the scene with an adult.

Let's make!

The more characters you make, the more fun you can have with your show. You could create puppets of your extended family, favourite celebrities or family pets. Create props by cutting out photographs or magazine snippets of objects (chairs, cars, toys etc.) then glue them onto card, folding the base to make it stand up.

If you liked making these, why not try making these other varieties of puppets? Finger or hand puppets can be made by cutting a basic silhouette of your character from two sheets of felt. Add simple features by gluing, drawing or sewing them onto the front, then sew together around the edges of the felt. You can also turn wooden spoons into puppets by adding googly eyes, painted-on features and felt accessories.

7 Attach the hands and feet onto the stick with paper fasteners. If the lollipop stick splits when you hammer the nail in, add the paper fastener then put a blob of glue over the back to secure the pin in place. Repeat Steps 5–7 for the right arm and leg.

8 To complete the puppet, glue the end of another lollipop stick to the back of the head.

Framed Puppet Theatre

This theatre is made from a picture frame and sets the stage for the family puppets on page 108. Decorated with pasta and gilded with gold paint, your mini maker can pull back the velvet curtains, shout 'Action!' and recreate your favourite family moments. You can use any size you like for the frame – just make sure all the measurements match up.

You will need

- 8 x 10in (20 x 25cm) picture frame, with glass and backing removed
- Macaroni or other small pasta shapes (approximately 60 pieces)
- Strong glue
- Gold acrylic paint
- Paintbrush
- 8 x 10in (20 x 25cm) purple velvet fabric
- 20in (50cm) gold rickrack

- Tailor's chalk or pencil
- 2 x eyelet hooks
- 16in (40cm) ribbon
- Sewing machine or needle and thread, pins
- Scrap of black card
- 2 x pieces of strong card, 8 x 12in (20 x 30cm)
- Scissors
- Mask template found on page 152

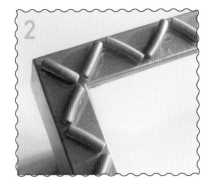

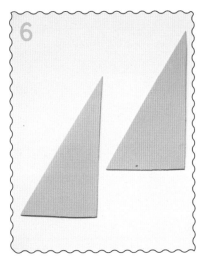

1 Begin by gluing the pasta around the front of the frame. Spread the glue in a zigzag pattern and arrange the pasta pieces on top. Do this in small sections at a time so the glue doesn't dry up before the pasta is positioned. Continue all around the frame and then leave it to set.

2 Paint the whole frame, including the pasta, with gold paint. You may need a few coats to get an even coverage.

3 To make the curtains, draw around the frame on the reverse of the fabric, using tailor's chalk or a pencil. Cut this out. Mark and cut the fabric down the centre, across the width to create the two curtains. If you want neat edges, fold the long sides under by ¼in (6mm) and sew. Repeat along the bottom edge.

4 To make the channel for the ribbon, fold down the top of each curtain by ¼in (6mm) to conceal the raw edges. Fold over again by 1in (2.5cm). Pin and sew along the fold with a sewing machine or by hand. Repeat this for the other curtain and feed the ribbon through both channels.

5 Screw on the eyelet hooks ½in (1cm) down from the top of the frame on the inside and tie the ribbon onto each one, with the front of the fabric at the front of the frame. Make sure it is tight so that the curtains don't droop.

6 To make the stands, measure the inside height of the frame and cut out two cardboard triangles to this height by 6in (15cm) wide. Paint them gold.

7 To make the curtain tie-backs, cut the length of gold rickrack in half. Then fold each piece down the middle and glue them into the inside rim of the frame in the centre, one on each side. Glue the cardboard stand on top of the tiebacks, using the photo as a reference.

8 For the theatre sign, draw around a teacup onto the strong card. Cut this out, then cut it in half and paint each piece gold on one side. Score a line ½in (1cm) from the straight edges on the gold side of each semi-circle and fold along the line. Glue the two circular sections together with wrong sides facing.

9 Use the template on page 152 to cut out two masks from black card. Paint a smiling face on one and a sad face on the other, using gold paint. Glue them onto one side of the semi-circles then glue the whole thing onto the top of the frame in the centre.

Let's play!

Use the Dancing Family Puppets on page 108 to act out your favourite family moments with this theatre as your stage.

Let's make!

Attaching pasta with glue is a great textural experience for children and there are lots of other things you could attach in the same way. Why not provide a selection in small bowls and let your child pick and choose? You could include other dried foods (such as rice, lentils or peas), beads, scraps of corrugated card, bolts or buttons. String is also fantastic for this because it can be moulded with the glue into swirling shapes.

If you want a quick, inexpensive theatre you could also make one from a cardboard shoebox. Cut one hole in the lid for the stage and another hole in the top so that you can fit the puppets through. Paint it gold and finish by attaching curtains to the back of the lid.

You could also extend the shoebox idea to make your very own easy shadow puppet theatre. Tape baking paper inside the lid and open up the back as well as the top. For the puppets, cut silhouettes from black card and attach them to lollipop sticks. Shine a torch through the back, turn down the lights, and let the performance begin!

Sewing and Stitching

To introduce sewing to children, it is a good idea to get them used to the process by using large plastic needles to thread string or embroidery thread onto lacing cards. You can then move onto smaller (but blunt) metal needles to sew basic patterns and attach pieces of felt together. Felt is a great for beginners as the fabric is inexpensive, colourful and has no right or wrong side.

You will need

- Large plastic and blunt metal needles
- Beginner 'threads' such as wool yarn, shoelaces and ribbon
- Fabric, plastic cross-stitch canvas, hole-punched paper plates, card and felt
- Embroidery hoop
- Long-reach, single-hole punch to allow you to create holes in card for thread

Simple sewing ideas

Family photos
A bit like join the dots with a needle. Print out family photos, punch holes and let children add colour or amusing accessories to the pictures through stitching.

Lacing cards
You can buy these or make your own by punching the outline of letters, shapes or words onto card for kids to sew with ribbon or wool yarn.

Teddy bear blanket set

Teach children the very basics of sewing with a machine by allowing them to sit on your lap and help guide the fabric while you sew basic items together, like a blanket for a teddy or doll. Pin together two squares of fabric, wrong sides together, and sew leaving a gap for turning at the bottom. Turn and stuff very lightly, then hand-sew together to make a small blanket and pillow.

First felt baubles

Circular pieces of felt can be stitched together with embroidery thread, decorated with sequins, glitter and beads and then hung onto a tree with some ribbon.

Felt toy

Children can draw out their own basic template of an animal onto paper. Be sure to keep the shape simple, bold and with no narrow sections (a cat, hedgehog or teddy shape would work well). Use the template to cut out two shapes from felt or fleece. Sew around the edges, leaving a 3in/8cm gap at the bottom, and fill with toy stuffing. Sew the gap up. Sew on buttons for eyes and glue or stitch on a simple nose and mouth.

Sewing tips

Be patient: sewing can be more time consuming than other crafts, and it may take a while to see the final picture. Kids may get bored easily so keep the projects simple.

Be prepared: create a sewing kit of supplies and keep scraps of fabric to practise on in a nice stitching bag (which you could make!).

Avoid tangles: keep threads within an arm's length when hand sewing – if the thread is too long, it will get tangled and take longer to sew, too short and you will be stopping and starting all the time.

Knot your thread: start and end hand sewing with a double knot to keep the stitches in place.

Little Stitchers

Stitching is a great way to develop motor skills and improve concentration. Younger kids can learn how to use a needle and thread with the sun and moon lacing project. The giant cross stitch takes a little patience, but makes a piece of art that will stand the test of time. Finally, the felt crown is an introduction to decorative embroidery stitches.

SKILLS LEARNED:
MOTOR SKILLS, CONCENTRATION,
GEOGRAPHICAL SKILLS, STITCHING
AND COORDINATION

Stitched Sun and Moon

This simple lacing project is a great introduction to stitching. Easy for little hands, lacing encourages children to understand sequences and develops hand–eye coordination. Mini makers can decorate the sun and moon and then stitch the sun's rays and nighttime stars. This project is great for helping to establish a morning and bedtime routine. Hang your sun and moon onto a bedroom wall or door and flip the sign around when it's day or night.

You will need

- 2 x paper plates, 9in (23cm) in diameter
- 3¼yd (3m) of ⅛in (4mm) wide yellow ribbon
- 3¼yd (3m) of ⅛in (4mm) wide silver ribbon
- Child's plastic needle
- Ruler
- Silver, yellow, pale blue and navy blue acrylic paint and paintbrush
- Black and red felt-tip pens

- Pencil
- Adhesive putty (such as Blu-Tak)
- Small bowl, about 5in (12.5cm) in diameter
- Lid or circular object with a 1in (2.5cm) diameter
- Hole punch
- Scissors
- Glue

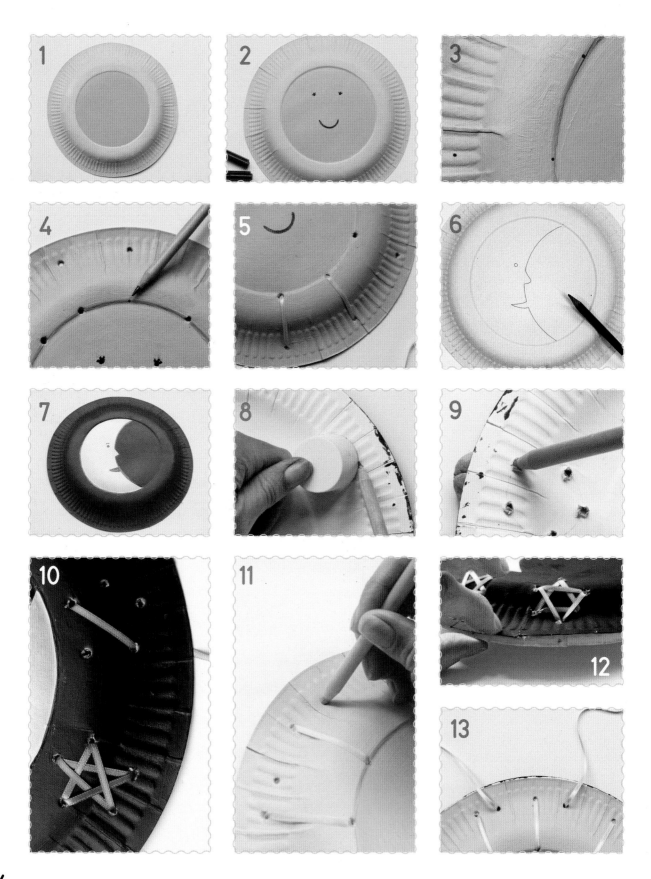

1 To make the daytime side, flip one plate over to the back and paint the circle in the middle yellow and the rest of the plate a pale blue. This may take a few coats to get an even coverage.

2 Once dry, use a black felt-tip pen to mark on some eyes, then use a red pen to draw on a little smiling mouth.

3 To mark the stitching holes, measure around the circumference of the sun with a ruler, putting a dot every 1½in (4cm) in pencil. Do this all the way around. From each mark, measure another 1½in (4cm) towards the edge of the plate and add another pencil dot.

4 Place a cherry-sized lump of adhesive putty underneath one of the pencil marks and poke through the plate with a pencil to make a hole big enough for the ribbon. Repeat for all the dots.

5 Tie a double knot in the end of the yellow ribbon. Thread it through the needle and begin stitching by feeding the ribbon through one of the holes around the edge of the sun, from the back. Thread it back through the corresponding hole near the rim and out through the next one along, continuing the process all around the sun. When you get to the end, tie another knot and cut away the excess ribbon.

6 For the nighttime side, take the other paper plate and place a small bowl (about 5in/12.5cm in diameter at the rim) over the back, so that it covers half of the circle in the centre of the plate. Draw around it in pencil to create a crescent shape. Add a nose, mouth and eyes.

7 Paint the moon silver and the rest of the plate navy blue. Once dry, outline the nose, mouth and eye with black pen.

8 Turn the plate over and use a pencil to draw around a lid on the rim of the plate, about ½in (1cm) from the edge. Repeat around the plate, so that you have about nine circles.

9 Mark five evenly spaced dots around each circle using a pencil. Place a piece of adhesive putty underneath each circle of five dots and poke through each one with a pencil, to make a hole. As this is from the back of the plate, you may need to re-poke the holes from the front so that they don't look messy.

10 Tie a double knot in the end of the silver ribbon and thread it through the needle. Feed the ribbon through one of the holes, from the back. Come back through, skipping one hole on the circle. Then skip another hole and go back through. Keep going, until you have created a star – you will have gone around the circle twice. Move on to the next circle, then work all the way around the plate.

11 Place the ruler in a straight line along the top of both the sun and moon, 1in (2.5cm) from the top. Measure the centre of this line then mark two points in pencil, 1in (2.5cm) from the centre on each side. With a piece of adhesive putty underneath, poke through the dots with a pencil.

12 Put a line of glue along the rim of one of the plates. Line up the punched holes then glue the plates together so that you have the sun on one side and the moon on the other.

13 Take 35in (90cm) of the remaining yellow ribbon, tie it into a double knot and thread it through one of the holes at the top and back through the other hole. Then tie the two ends with a double knot and pull the thread so you have two loops to hang over the door.

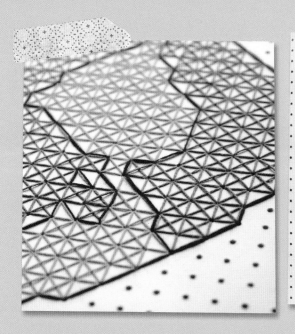
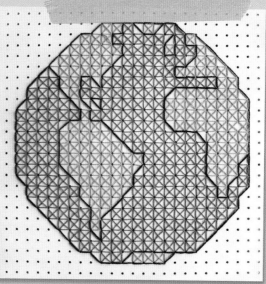

Giant Cross Stitch Art

This woolly map of the world is stitching on a large scale! It makes a fantastic piece of art for a bedroom and is a straightforward sewing project as the holes are large and easy to thread through. We've included a pattern for this one, if you need it, but getting kids to draw out their own map would be a fantastic way to learn about the world. The world map will take a few hours to finish, so if you're after a quicker project, use a smaller board and a simpler design. Draw it onto squared paper before transferring onto the board.

You will need

- 20in (50cm) square white pegboard

- 1 x 25g ball of yarn in blue, green and black

- Child's plastic needle

- Pencil

- Scissors

- Paper fastener or split pin (if not using pattern provided)

- Tape measure (if not using pattern provided)

- Squared paper (if not using pattern provided)

- Cross-stitch pattern, found on page 129 (optional)

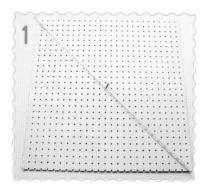

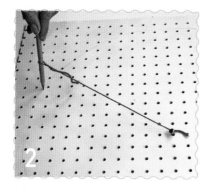

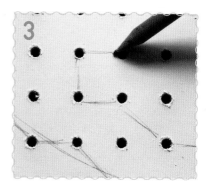

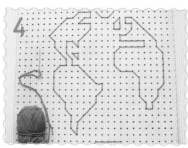

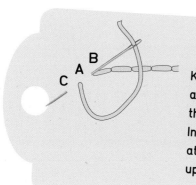

1 If you would like to use the pattern on page 129 to create the cross stitch, skip straight to step 3. To draw your own, begin by finding the centre point of the board. Place a tape measure diagonally across the pegboard from corner to corner. Place a paper fastener in the nearest hole to the centre.

2 Tie a 12in (30cm) strand of yarn under the head of the paper fastener. Measure out 8in (20cm) along from the pin and tie a pencil onto the yarn at this length. Use the pencil as a compass to draw a large circle on the board. Remove the pin and discard the yarn.

3 Look at a world map for guidance and pencil out the shapes of the continents onto the board. With a rough shape drawn out, you just need to go over the pencil lines, connecting the holes in the board nearest to each line. You can also draw this onto squared paper first if you like, just count up the holes making up the height and width of the board and draw a box to this size. Transfer the lines onto the board from your pattern. If you want to use the stitch pattern provided on page 129, mark out the outlines shown onto the board in pencil.

4 Pull an arm's length of green yarn and put a double-knot in the end. Stitch the outline of the countries using backstitch (see box below). When you reach the end of the yarn, secure it with a double knot at the back of the board and start again.

5 When all the countries are outlined, backstitch the remainder of the globe circle using blue thread. Working around the board, fill in all the outlined continents in green and all the sea area in blue using cross stitch (see box opposite). Don't stitch across any existing diagonal stitches as this will affect the shape of the outline. After each cross stitch, sew a box around it using backstitch.

Backstitch

Knot the end of the thread and bring the needle in through the back of the fabric at A. Insert it back in to the right at B. Bring the needle back up at C. Repeat this process.

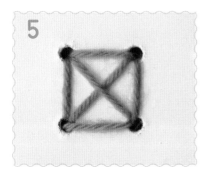

5

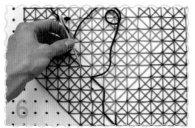

6

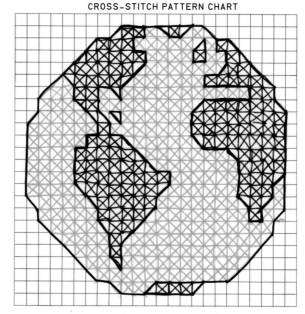

6 Finally, go around the outline of the countries to make them stand out against the sea. Sew each of them in black yarn, using backstitch.

Cross stitch

Knot the end of the thread and push the needle through the back of the fabric. Insert the needle back through the fabric as if making a diagonal running stitch. Make another stitch going diagonally across the original, as though you are sewing from corner to corner of a square.

Let's make!

If you want a quicker project, why not try stitching a starry scene, such as your star sign or a favourite constellation? Just stitch crosses for the stars and connect them with backstitch. You could also stitch your name or another word to create a lovely personalized door sign. Most basic scenes can be stitched onto a pegboard, as long as the shapes are relatively large and simple. A stitched picture of a rainbow, a favourite animal or even your house would all make great pieces of art. You can also try stitching onto furniture, using chairs with a wicker seat panel or even adding an edging to shoes or clothing.

Felt Crown

This reversible felt crown is the perfect topper for any royal outfit. It's made from felt and embellished with simple stitching, with elastic to ensure it stays happily on your head. Felt is a great first fabric for kids as it's cheap, doesn't fray and is easy to work with. You could also glue embellishments on – stick-on gems, pompoms, sequins and glitter glue work well. Use as part of the dressing-up kit in the next chapter (see page 136).

You will need

- 8 x 12in (20 x 30cm) pieces of felt in two colours

- 8 x 12in (20 x 30cm) fusible webbing

- Pencil or fabric pen

- Embroidery thread in four colours

- Embroidery needle

- Eyelet kit with two ¼in (6mm) eyelets

- Pins

- Hammer

- 18in (45cm) length of elastic, ¹⁄₁₆in (2mm) wide

- Thin pressing cloth

- Scissors

- Hole punch

- Crown template, found on page 156

- Iron and ironing board

1 Photocopy and cut out the template from page 156. Remember to cut out the three diamond shapes too. Place the template on top of both felt pieces, pin it in place, then cut it out. To cut out the diamonds from the felt, fold the section in half and make a little snip in the folded fabric to get the cutting started.

2 To embroider the crown, transfer the stitch pattern from the template onto your piece of felt using pencil or fabric pen. If you prefer, you can draw out your own design onto the paper template to practise, then use a pencil or fabric pen to lightly mark the design directly onto the felt.

3 Stitch the design onto both pieces of felt using running stitch (see box opposite) and cross stitch (see box on page 129). Secure with a knot at the back and trim off any excess thread.

4 To attach the two pieces of felt together, pin the fusible webbing to the back of one of them. Cut around it to create a crown shape from the webbing. Sandwich the webbing between the two crown pieces, with wrong sides together, on an ironing board. Cover with a thin pressing cloth then press with an iron to fuse the pieces, following the manufacturer's guidelines.

5 If the felt pieces do not match up perfectly, snip away any excess with scissors. Be careful not to cut through any of the stitches.

6 Use a hole punch to make a hole at both edges, approximately ½in (1cm) from each end of the crown. Insert the eyelets and hammer them together, following the manufacturer's instructions.

7 Thread one end of the elastic through one of the eyelets then through the other. Tie a loose knot in the two ends. You should have two lines of elastic at the back with the knot in one of them. See if it fits your child and adjust it accordingly. It should fit onto the head above the ears so it doesn't fall down over the face.

Let's make!

This crown is a great addition to any dressing-up box as it's made to last and the elastic can be adjusted to fit different-sized heads. However, if you're looking for a really quick crown make, you could just cut felt, foam or cardboard to fit your child's head and tape together. This can then be decorated with pompoms, cotton wool, sequins, gems and anything else you can lay your hands on. It's also a great activity for a majestic party or play date. Twisting together pipe cleaners works well for a more dainty-looking crown.

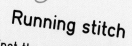

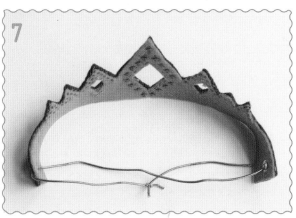

Running stitch

Knot the end of the thread and push the needle through the back of the fabric. Insert the needle back in just to the left or right of where the thread came through and pull taught. The stitch can be as long as you like, about ¼in (6mm) would suit this project. Repeat all along the line you want to stitch.

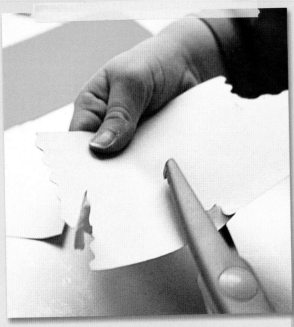

Cutting and Sticking

While encouraging children to handle a pair of scissors can be a daunting prospect for a parent, it really doesn't need to be. Child-friendly scissors are nowhere near as scary as adult ones and teaching kids how to use them is an excellent way to develop hand–eye coordination, fine motor skills and improve concentration. Creating collages is a fun activity and there are so many things you could use to make them, giving a lot of scope for variation. Keep a stash of old magazines, wrapping paper, fabric scraps and so on, so you always have things on hand for sticking.

You will need

- Child-friendly scissors with a variety of different-shaped blades (you can get zigzag, wavy and loads of other shapes from craft stores)

- Solvent-free glue, PVA and glue sticks

- Glue spreader or paintbrushes

- Glue pot

- Tapes: sticky tape, decorative tape and duct tape are all fantastic for crafting

- Sticky-back plastic

Cutting and sticking ideas

Pasta pictures

Use big dollops of PVA glue to stick various pasta shapes onto card to make pictures. You can even dye the pasta in a variety of colours beforehand (see the method used on page 148). Or, paint the pasta on the card, once it is dry.

Window sun catchers

Place a cut-out paper frame onto some sticky-back plastic (sticky side up) and let kids stick cut-up tissue paper onto the plastic until it's full up. Attach it onto the window and wait for the sunshine to appear and shine through it.

Papier mâché

This is a fun craft technique that can be used as a base for creating some fantastic things. Follow the instructions for the banjo on page 67 to build up layers of torn paper to create texture and give strength to objects.

Dancing paper dolls

Fold a long strip of paper in a concertina fashion, draw on a silhouette of a person (with the hands going all the way to the fold), then snip out and unfold. Embellish each doll with card scraps.

Collage

Use child-friendly scissors with different shaped blades to cut scraps of paper, thin plastic, bubble wrap and tin foil for your collage and add a range of other items to create texture and pattern. Bottle tops, sequins, pompoms, feathers, ribbon, buttons and so on are all great. Use ample PVA glue to enable them to stick and create your collage on card for stability.

Magnets

It may be a different kind of sticking, but magnets offer a whole host of re-stickable craft activities and we love them – as you can see by the selection included within this book! Glue paper onto magnetic sheets so that children can draw, colour and cut out their own fridge magnets.

Cutting and sticking tips

Aprons on: as with most craft, sticking can be a messy affair, especially with papier mâché, so make sure everyone involved is well covered.

Teach by example: encourage safe and proper use of scissors and show children how to hold and use them. Explain what you're doing so they can copy and learn.

Dressing Up

These projects show you how to create costume items for crafty kings and queens, but you can transfer the basic principles of each project to make a range of other dressing-up pieces. The robe is so easy to make and it can easily be transformed to make any other style of cape you can possibly think of – from superheroes to snow queens.

SKILLS LEARNED:
SEWING, IMAGINARY PLAY AND BAKING

Edible Magic Wands

These delicious edible wands add a finishing flourish to the royal outfit you can learn to make in this chapter. They are a magical project to encourage mini makers to become little kitchen helpers. They can get involved in the whole process – weighing and mixing the ingredients, using the cookie cutters and decorating the wands.

You will need

To make 12–15 wands:

- Star-shaped metal cookie cutter, 2¹/₂in (6cm) in diameter

- 1¹/₂oz (45g) butter

- 10¹/₂oz (300g) mini white and pink marshmallows

- 6¹/₂oz (180g) crispy rice cereal

- 3¹/₂oz (100g) white chocolate

- Edible glitter

- 8 x wooden skewers, 10in (25cm) long

- Baking paper

- Baking tray, measuring 13¹/₂ x 8 x 1¹/₂in (34 x 20 x 4cm)

1 Begin by melting the butter in a saucepan over a low heat. Add the marshmallows to the melted butter and cook gently until they are melted, stirring constantly.

2 Take the saucepan off the heat, pour into a large mixing bowl, add the rice cereal and stir the mixture until all the cereal is covered.

3 Press the mixture into a tray lined with baking paper. Place another sheet of baking paper over the top and press down until it is flattened and compressed. Put the mixture in the fridge for an hour to set.

4 Once the mixture has hardened, use a cookie cutter to cut the crispy mixture into stars. Push a skewer into each star.

5 Melt the white chocolate in a bowl over a saucepan of boiling water and leave to cool a little.

6 To decorate, place the wands onto a piece of baking paper and use a teaspoon to carefully drizzle the white chocolate on top. Leave to cool and harden, then dust on a little glitter for some extra sparkle and magic!

Let's make!

You can create different-shaped wands by using a variety of cookie cutters – just make sure the cutter isn't too big or they will become top heavy. You could even make smaller shapes and thread them onto thin elastic for an edible necklace. Yummy!

Easy Royal Robe

This robe is made from red polar fleece and finished with a fluffy white trim and monogrammed crown motif. This project involves some basic sewing, which can easily be done on a machine or by hand.

You will need

- 1 x 1yd (1 x 1m) red polar fleece

- 1yd (1m) length of 1½in (4cm) wide red ribbon

- Strip of white furry fabric, 5 x 46in (12.5 x 116cm)

- Approximately 35 x black sequins, ¼in (6mm) in diameter

- White sewing thread, needle and pins

- Tape measure

- Tailor's chalk or pen

- Strong glue

- Safety pin

- 5 x 6in (12.5 x 15cm) yellow felt

- Scrap of purple felt

- Fusible webbing and an iron

- Tweezers

- Scissors

- Template of crown shape, found on page 156

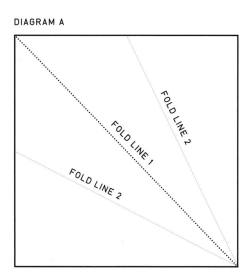

1 Fold the polar fleece fabric in half diagonally, then fold this in half again (see diagram A).

2 At the narrowest point, cut off 6in (15cm) from the end. At the widest end, cut along the existing straight raw edge. This should be visible on the top layer of the folded fabric (see diagram B). Open up the fabric.

3 Cut 12in (30cm) off the end of the strip of furry fabric and set this aside for the collar. Measure and cut the remaining fur in half down the length to create two strips measuring 34 x 2½in (86 x 6cm). Pin fur trim down both straight sides of the fabric (on the right side). Then sew in place.

4 Glue the sequins down the centre of both pieces of fur trim, spacing them about 2in (5cm) apart. To easily apply the sequins, use tweezers to dip them into the glue and place them onto the fur trim.

DIAGRAM A

FOLD LINE 2
FOLD LINE 1
FOLD LINE 2

DIAGRAM B

CUT LINE

5 Take the piece of fur you set aside for the collar. Fold it in half lengthways, then place it over the top of the robe, sandwiching in the fleece fabric. Pin and sew ¼in (6mm) from the bottom of the trim, making sure you incorporate both sides of the trim with your needle.

6 Take the red ribbon and attach a safety pin onto one end. Feed it through the fur trim channel at the top of the robe to make the ties.

7 Photocopy and cut out the template from page 156 and use it to cut one crown shape from yellow felt and one from fusible webbing. Also cut out your child's first initial from the scrap of purple felt and fusible webbing. Make sure this letter is small enough to fit inside the crown piece.

8 Lay the back of the robe out right side up and measure 10in (25cm) from the top. Place the tape measure horizontally across and mark the centre point. Mark this point in pen or tailor's chalk.

9 Place the felt crown and webbing onto the fleece where marked, with the fusible webbing carefully sandwiched between the felt and fleece. Use a warm iron to fuse the crown in place, following the manufacturer's instructions for the webbing. Then place the letter pieces onto the crown and repeat the process to fuse the felt in place. Finally, to embellish, glue black sequins onto the tips of the crown.

Let's make!

This easy-sew cape forms a fantastic basis for lots of quick costume ideas made from fleece. Use green fleece and create a dragon cape by sewing spikes down the back and adding a simple tail. Add a fin to grey fleece to create a shark costume and make a witch cape by embellishing black fleece with sparkly rickrack. Finally, add a superhero symbol to a red cape and pair with tights worn underneath a pair of pants and you're ready to save the world!

Rainbow Pasta Necklace

This medallion necklace made from salt dough and dyed pasta is the perfect finishing touch to a royal dressing-up outfit. It's really simple to make and kids will love getting their hands messy making the salt dough, designing the stamp and threading it all together.

You will need

For the pasta beads:

- Food colouring in four contrasting colours

- 1³/₄oz (50g) mix of dried pasta tubes such as penne or macaroni

- 3¹/₂ fl oz (100ml) bottle of sanitizing hand gel

- 4 x zip-lock bags

- Baking tray lined with baking paper

- 4 x cocktail sticks

For the salt-dough pendant:

- 1³/₄oz (50g) salt

- 1³/₄oz (50g) flour

- 1¹/₄ fl oz (35ml) lukewarm water

- Tray lined with baking paper

- Scrap of corrugated cardboard

- Rolling pin

- 2¹/₂in (6cm) circular cookie cutter

- Cling film

- Gold acrylic paint and paintbrush

- ¹/₂in (1cm) pony beads (approximately 40)

- 18in (46cm) length of narrow elastic

- Template for the stamp, found on page 152

- Pencil

1 Place two teaspoons of hand gel into a zip-lock bag. Add a small amount of food colouring with a cocktail stick and close the bag, making sure to remove as much air as possible. Mix the liquids together with your fingers, until they are fully blended. The colour should be the same brightness you'd like the beads to be. If needed, add more food colouring until you are happy with the colour.

2 Open the bag and add a quarter of the pasta to it, making sure you get a mix of the different pasta shapes. Reclose the bag and shake the pasta to move it around in the coloured mixture. Keep doing so until it is completely covered with the dye. Set to one side.

3 Repeat steps 1 and 2 with the three other colours to make a selection of pasta beads. Split the remaining pasta equally into three bags. Leave the pasta in the bag until you have the colour you desire. This could take up to an hour to get an even colour. The longer you leave it in there, the more vibrant the colour will become.

4 Line a baking tray with baking paper and tip the pasta onto it. They will still be wet from the dye but the excess liquid will be absorbed. Put each colour into a different part of the tray, being careful not to let the different colours touch.

5 Leave the pasta to dry overnight, then store them in an airtight container.

Pasta-dying tips

Make sure the zip-lock bags are sealed without much air trapped inside or it will be tricky to get a good coverage of the dye onto the pasta shapes.

Get kids to help squish the pasta around in the dye to colour them.

6 For the salt-dough pendant, begin by making the crown stamp. Photocopy and cut out the template from page 152 then use it to cut out a crown shape from corrugated cardboard. You could also design your own stamp – just make sure it is simple, easy to cut out from card and around 1in (2.5cm) in size.

7 Preheat the oven to 210°F/100°C/ Gas Mark ¼. Mix the salt and flour together in a bowl until they are combined. Add the lukewarm water in small amounts at a time and mix together to create a dough-like consistency. If the dough is too sticky add more flour, or if it's too crumbly add more water.

8 Transfer the dough onto a cling-film covered surface and use a rolling pin to roll it out a little. Place the cardboard stamp on top and roll it into the dough until it is about ¼in (6mm) thick. Remove the card to reveal an imprint of the crown.

9 Place the circular cutter on top of the dough with the crown print in the centre. Cut out the circle and give it a little twist to make sure the edges are neat.

10 Transfer the pendant onto a baking tray lined with baking paper and use a pencil to pierce a small hole ¼in (6mm) from the top, to enable you to thread it onto the necklace. Bake for 2–3 hours, turning halfway through until the dough is hard. Once cooked, remove from the oven and leave to cool.

11 Paint the pendant gold. It may take several coats to cover it evenly.

Working with salt dough

Salt dough can be made really quickly from things you're likely to have in your food cupboard already. The dough can also be stored in an air-tight container for up to a week in the fridge, making it an ideal last-minute activity for bored kids. You can cut shapes with cookie cutters and turn them into wands or make hanging decorations and pendants, like we have here. Bear in mind, the dough takes at least a couple of hours to bake, so have an activity lined up while you wait. Once baked, you can decorate salt dough with paint and embellish with sequins, glitter, buttons and countless other things. Take care if you want to varnish the finished product as some types don't react well with the salt. Do a small tester first to be sure.

Let's make!

This idea can be extended to fit lots of different themes or interests. You could use yellow and black pasta with a dinosaur footprint pendant for a caveman. Or, use a pen lid to stamp Olympic rings onto the dough and glue it to a piece of red ribbon to create a medal. You could then paint them gold, silver and bronze and host your own sports day!

Making jewellery with pre-dyed pasta is a great activity to do with a group of friends, or as a party activity. Younger children can glue the rainbow pasta onto paper to create pictures, while older kids thread their pieces together. Having several colours also makes a great sorting or colour-matching activity for tiny tots.

12 Thread the length of elastic through the hole in the pendant. Then tie a knot so the elastic is secured at the top of the pendant.

13 Thread the dyed pasta and the pony beads onto the elastic in any order you like.

14 Once you've filled up each side of the necklace finish with a pony bead and tie a double knot in the end. Tie the two ends of the elastic together.

Templates

Sticky-felt Hanging Calendar photocopy at 100%

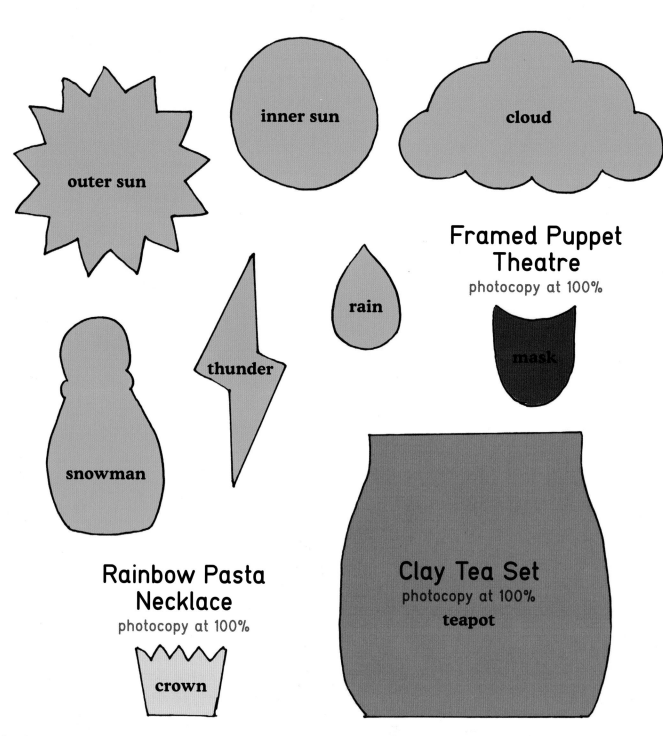

outer sun

inner sun

cloud

Framed Puppet Theatre
photocopy at 100%

rain

thunder

mask

snowman

Rainbow Pasta Necklace
photocopy at 100%

crown

Clay Tea Set
photocopy at 100%

teapot

Cardboard Anchor

photocopy at 165%

Magnetic Family
Faces Accessories
photocopy at 120%

Family Fishing Game photocopy at 150%

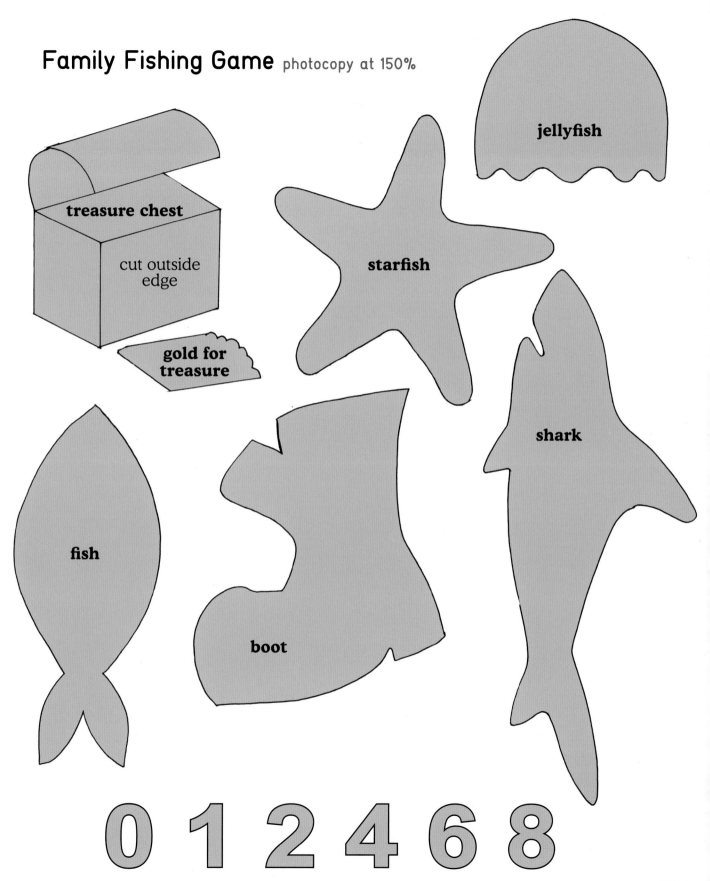

treasure chest

cut outside edge

gold for treasure

starfish

jellyfish

shark

fish

boot

0 1 2 4 6 8

Easy Royal Robe
photocopy at 125%

crown

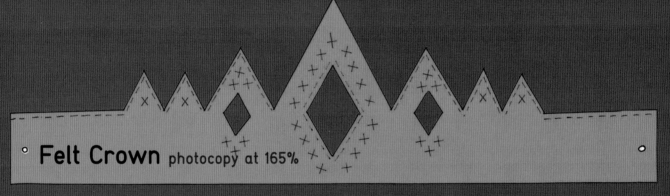

Felt Crown photocopy at 165%

Pebble Dominoes
photocopy at 100%

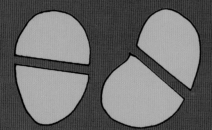

star

Paper-plate Tambourine
photocopy at 200%

Suppliers

UK

www.hobbycraft.co.uk
For a huge range of craft items

www.kobrapaint.com
For acrylic spray paints

www.theworks.co.uk
Great for budget craft supplies
for kids' projects

www.etsy.com
For unique, specialist and handmade items

www.candh.co.uk
Great for a large range of fabrics to suit
all budgets

www.johnlewis.com
Reliable and great for fabrics

www.tigerstores.co.uk
An excellent resource for cheap
craft supplies.

US

www.michaels.com
www.joann.com
www.acmoore.com
www.hobbylobby.com
For a huge range of craft items

About us

We are two best friends, mothers, crafters and writers living in Brighton, UK. Both of us have been crafting ever since we were little and have happy memories of sticking toilet rolls together and making all sorts of masterpieces with our own parents. Now that we have little ones ourselves, we spend all of our time trying to think of new things to make with them. We began our blog, *Little Button Diaries*, as a way of documenting all the things we got up to. It quickly became an obsession and we love being able to dedicate time to making things for, and with, our children. We also wanted to show that, while becoming a mum takes over every spare second of your time, there is always room for crafting and a lot can be achieved, even if you only have 30 minutes, a bag of pasta and some PVA glue to hand. We hope you enjoy the projects in this book as much as we enjoyed making them and testing them out on our own Little Buttons.

**Visit www.littlebuttondiaries.com for loads of ideas
to make and bake for and with your children.**

Authors' acknowledgements

The projects in this book have been tried and tested by our own Little Buttons: Harper, Grayson, Amelie and Lilah. We love you all very much, and thank you for constantly inspiring us to make things. Big thanks also to our partners Nick and George, who have been ever supportive and patient when their houses became stuffed full with glitter, paint and washi tape! x

Publisher's acknowledgements

GMC Publications would like to thank our lovely models: Harper, Bea, Jack, Amelie, Joshua, Lilah, Grayson, Beau and Cressida. Thanks also to Collette and Stephanie at the Paddock Art Studios, Lewes.

Photo credits

Page 45: Shutterstock, Jessica Torres Photography
Page 145 (bottom right): Chris Gloag

Index

To place an order, or to request a catalogue, contact:
GMC Publications Ltd, Castle Place, 166 High Street, Lewes,
East Sussex, BN7 1XU, United Kingdom
Tel: +44 (0)1273 488005   www.gmcbooks.com